Continuing
Professional Development
2nd edition

David Megginson is Professor of HRD at Sheffield Hallam University. He has been on the Membership and Education Committee of CIPD and remains on the CPD Working Group.

Vivien Whitaker lectures, researches and consults at Sheffield Hallam University.

The Chartered Institute of Personnel and Development is the leading publisher of books and reports for personnel and training professionals, students, and for all those concerned with the effective management and development of people at work. For details of all titles, please contact the Publishing Department:

tel: 020 8612 6204
email publish@cipd.co.uk
The catalogue of all CIPD titles can be viewed on the CIPD website:
www.cipd.co.uk/bookstore

Continuing
Professional Development
2nd edition

David Megginson
and
Vivien Whitaker

Chartered Institute of Personnel and Development

Published by the Chartered Institute of Personnel and Development,
151 The Broadway, Wimbledon, London SW19 1JQ

First edition published 2003
Reprinted 2004, 2005
Second edition published 2007
Reprinted 2007, 2008, 2009

Design by Fakenham Photosetting, Fakenham, Norfolk
Typeset by Kerrypress Ltd, Luton, Bedfordshire
Printed in Great Britain by Short Run Press Limited, Exeter

British Library Cataloguing in Publication Data
A catalogue of this publication is available from the British Library

ISBN 1 84398 166 1
ISBN-13 978 1 84398 166 4

Charted Institute of Personnel and Development
151 The Broadway, Wimbledon, London SW19 1JQ
Tel: 020 8612 6200
E-mail: cipd@cipd.co.uk   website: www.cipd.co.uk
Incorporated by Royal Charter.   Registered Charity No. 1079797

Contents

Acknowledgements   ix

List of figures   xi

Preface   xiii

PART 1 EXPLORING CONTINUING PROFESSIONAL DEVELOPMENT   **1**

1 Clarifying Continuing Professional Development   3
    Introduction
    The need for CPD
    Core concepts of CPD
    Stakeholders involved in CPD
    Key principles of CPD
    Giving priority to CPD
    Transforming limitations to CPD
    The relevance of CPD
    Conclusion

2 Understanding Continuing Professional Development   19
    Introduction
    The seven paradoxes within CPD
    The paradoxes explored
    Conclusion – developing a high level of curiosity

PART 2 ENGAGING IN CONTINUING PROFESSIONAL DEVELOPMENT   **27**

3 Identifying development needs   29
    Introduction
    Developing an 'extraordinarily realistic self-image'
    Sources of a sense of self
    Framework for developing an ERSI
    Specific work-based issues
    Development issues emerging from reflection
    Feedback from others
    Self-assessment metrics
    Organisational metrics
    Professional standards
    Conclusion – the agenda for change

4 Prioritising needs and selecting appropriate activities   51
    Introduction
    Summarise your development agenda
    Balanced goals
    Goals and plans
    Goal-setting theory

Priorities – the final check
Formats for your CPD plan
Putting it all together – staring up the steps

5 Undertaking development activities   69
  Introduction
  Being a skilled learner
  Methods of development
  The range of methods
  Getting the most out of the experiences we have (FAQs)
  Conclusion

6 Recording and evaluating development   87
  Introduction
  Reasons for recording
  The CPD record
  Logging reflection and reviewing
  Why does journal-writing work?
  A portfolio of action and learning
  Evaluation of CPD
  The CIPD's stance on recording
  Conclusion

PART 3 CONSOLIDATING YOUR CPD ACHIEVEMENTS   **101**

7 Celebrating success   103
  Introduction
  Finishing the fringe
  Owning our success
  Acknowledging and thanking people who helped
  Addressing the demonic aspect
  Letting go of excess baggage
  Being authentic
  Celebrating completion
  Spreading the word
  Conclusion

8 Networking your future   115
  Introduction
  Analysing your CPD network
  Creating a learning network through Action Learning
  Creating your own self-development group
  Learning partners – mentoring
  Five degrees of separation
  How to organise and encourage CPD
  Conclusion

9 Empowering career creativity   127
    Introduction
    Using our senses to enhance our learning
    CPD for visually-oriented learners
    Tuning in for auditorily-oriented learners
    Getting a hold on kinaesthetically-oriented learning
    Further refining our skills in analysis and planning
    Conclusion
    Appendix 1   143
    Appendix 2   146

    Resources and bibliography   147

    Index   153

Acknowledgements

We owe special thanks to:

All our students on various MSc programmes – especially HRM, HRD, Outdoor Management Development, IT & Management, Mentoring & Coaching and other professionals who have shared their CPD experiences with us

Our colleagues at Sheffield Hallam University, especially Colin Beard, David Clutterbuck, Godfrey Craik, Katherine Gardiner, Lynne Booth, Bob Garvey, Toby Rhodes and Paul Stokes, who have worked with us in designing CPD processes; we are also grateful to Andrew Rothwell who we encountered on the CIPD's CPD website discussion forum, and who generously led us to his own and others' recent research in this field

Members of the CIPD's Membership and Education Committee and CPD Working Party for their fascination with CPD and their support for our work on this book; while so many of the members have been helpful we would like to acknowledge a particular debt and thanks to Noël Baker, Jean Floodgate, Steve Rogers and Diane Warren

CIPD members at branch, regional and national events who have shared their wisdom and experience

Christine Williams and her colleagues at CIPD House, for their challenging and supportive engagement with this project

Chris Swift and Joan Butt for the illustrations

Robert Foss, for asking us to write this book, advising on style and encouraging us to write about our practice

Ruth Lake, our editor, for her efficiency, clarity and flexibility

Our reviewers for their full and generous feedback, which helped to shape the book

Ed, for being cheerful and cool and for putting up with us during the delivery

List of figures

1 The CPD cycle   27

2 Framework for developing an ERSI   31

3 Map of career metaphors   35

4 Fishbone for Tom's world class me   52

5 Detail of areas under 'Colleague' in Tom's fishbone   52

6 Planned and emergent learning strategies   59

7 Modes of development   61

8 The components of emotional intelligence   74

9 Evaluation framework for an expedition   97

10 Strandgaard's model of change   108

11 Current state of metaphorical house   109

12 Desired state of metaphorical house   109

13 Extract from a Rich Picture of an HR trainer   129

14 Learning map of an assistant HR manager   131

15 Planning using the metaphor of a roundabout   133

16 Model of Damien's working environment as a new member of
   the training team   135

17 Model of how Damien would like the dynamics of the training team to be   136

18 Part of a Post-It brainstorm for a Learning and Development manager   137

Preface

This is a book about recognising, releasing and realising potential.

Its purpose is to explore the importance of Continuing Professional Development (CPD), to explain the relevance of CPD to a range of different people and to expand on the excitement that engaging in CPD can engender.

This book recognises that if we are to maximise our enjoyment of work and life we need to be continually responding to the changing world we live in: are you living to work or working to live? What would you like to be doing? We need to look within at our latent skills and abilities and explore ways of building on our current talents and developing new aspects of ourselves.

Part 1 explains the importance of CPD. Part 2 explores the different methods that can be used to analyse development needs and create and implement a CPD plan. Part 3 assists in recognising and building on success and examines creative ways of engaging in CPD planning, so that it need never become repetitious.

This is a sequel to our book on Cultivating Self-Development (Megginson and Whitaker, 1996) and is written in a similar style, encouraging the reader to reflect on their professional career and engage in activities as they progress through the text. It is based on our experience of working with people on their CPD over the past 20 years.

This book is designed to assist a number of groups of readers. These are listed below.

Full-time and part-time students

CIPD students undertaking the Professional Development Scheme will find this an essential core text for their studies. A tutor manual that supports the text is available for lecturers.

The introduction of student progress files for undergraduate students provides a framework for them to log both their self-reflection and their professional progress. This book provides them with frameworks to develop their professional planning beyond the duration of their formal course and to assist them to focus and develop their career. Postgraduate students will also benefit from such guidance.

All undergraduate and postgraduate students need to develop skills in critical reasoning as part of academic study. The theoretical dialogues within this text are designed to encourage this crucial ability.

Members of the Chartered Institute of Personnel and Development (CIPD)

The CIPD requires its members to formalise their interest and commitment to CPD by creating and implementing a CPD plan every year. As a CIPD member you may already be convinced of the benefits of CPD, so you may choose to focus on Parts 2 and 3 of the book.

Individuals interested in developing themselves

Although this book is primarily designed for members or potential members of the CIPD, and many of the examples are of HR professionals, the principles and practices we discuss are useful for anyone interested in CPD.

Employers/HR managers

This is also a book for employers and HR managers who are seeking to learn of the benefits of encouraging their staff to focus on CPD.

We have worked with a wide range of PLCs and public sector organisations in implementing and evaluating CPD programmes. Results have shown that CPD helps to increase job satisfaction, retain professional staff, enhance succession planning and assist staff to cope with the challenges of change.

Preface to the 2nd edition

In this edition we have sought to do three things, while not making major changes to the form of the book and the bulk of its content. We have:

- added to the commentary on critical debates in CPD, and pointed to new references to research in this area

- suggested at various points in the text how CPD might be encouraged and organised by HR professionals

- given examples of how senior members of the profession might engage in CPD and take benefits from the process.

We would value feedback from readers and will seek to incorporate what we learn from it into any subsequent editions of the book that might be published in the future. Please respond with suggestions to:

d.f.megginson@shu.ac.uk

or, even better (if you are a CIPD member), add to the discussion forum in the CPD community space at:

www.cipd.co.uk/communities/discussions

Exploring Continuing Professional Development

We start by engaging in the essential practical and theoretical exploration of Continuing Professional Development.

This will assist you to orient yourself to this subject and, in the course of doing so, will get you started on considering your own professional progress.

Within these two chapters are a series of questionnaires and activities. We encourage you to start a personal CPD log and include your responses to these exercises within it.

This log will help you to crystallise and summarise your view of CPD and link your learning from Part 1 to the range of activities in Parts 2 and 3 of this book.

In Part 2, the chapters are structured to take the reader through a development cycle. Chapter 3 focuses on assessing your current CPD agenda. Chapter 4 explores where you want to be. Chapter 5 looks pragmatically at action to achieve your aim and Chapter 6 helps you to review and evaluate your progress.

Part 3 will assist you in recognising and consolidating your CPD successes. It offers suggestions for increasing your networks and experimenting with a variety of methods for analysis and planning for your next cycle of CDP.

Clarifying Continuing
Professional Development

INTRODUCTION

Continuing Professional Development (CPD) is a process by which individuals take control of their own learning and development, by engaging in an on-going process of reflection and action. This process is empowering and exciting and can stimulate people to achieve their aspirations and move towards their dreams.

CPD provides the opportunity to soar like an eagle or a helicopter and look at our career progress from a wider perspective. It challenges us to make time for regular personal reflection and review. It reminds us that we have the responsibility for developing ourselves rather than pushing the onus on to our manager or others in the organisation.

Remember the old saying, 'You can take a horse to water but you can't make it drink'? Our response to that is to say that CPD is about becoming thirsty – thirsty for new knowledge, thirsty for new skills, thirsty for new experiences.

THE NEED FOR CPD

The need for CPD arises because security for individuals no longer lies in the job or organisation we work for but in the skills, knowledge and experience that we have within ourselves.

Authoritative reports (Institute for Employment Studies – Tamkin *et al*, 1995; Industrial Relations Services, 1998; Income Data Services, 1999) highlight CPD as a major intervention that we can make into our own development.

CORE CONCEPTS OF CPD

What makes CPD different from other types of training and development?

1 The learner is in control – CPD starts from the learner's dream.

2 CPD is a holistic process and can address all aspects of life and the balance between them.

3 Regularly looking forward to how we want to be, reflecting on how we are, and working from our present position towards the future direction, helps in achieving CPD's purposes and adds zest and direction to work and learning.

4 CPD works if you have the support and financial backing of your employer, and it also works even if the employer is indifferent or hostile.

CPD is not a panacea – like anything else it must be looked at in relation to the rest of the individual's life, the organisational context and the wider work environment.

STAKEHOLDERS INVOLVED IN CPD

There are several parties with an interest or stake in CPD. Centrally, there is yourself. We have written this book with the firm conviction that CPD works for individuals, and that it makes complete sense to engage with the process whether you are under pressure to do it from others or not.

Others are also arguing that CPD is important for you. Many employers see it as crucial to development. They use CPD as a means of giving power and focus to a range of HRD interventions.

Universities and colleges also use CPD to help learners link their curriculum to the relevant and often pressing concerns of current work, or their future career. Academic institutions also develop CPD in response to the requirements of professional bodies. These bodies advocate it as a way of supporting their members and as a means to underpin individual Charter membership.

The benefits of CPD for individuals

As individuals, many of us may not have had appropriate careers advice when young or may have jumped at the first job on offer. In the rush of our day-to-day existence we may not have given ourselves the chance to reflect and consider whether we are getting what we want in our professional lives.

> Sadler Smith *et al*, 2000, found that the three main benefits of CPD for individuals were updating (maintenance), competence (survival) and enhanced mobility. How does this accord with your motives or those discussed elsewhere in this chapter?

The benefits of CPD for employers

Employers are increasingly concerned that employees undertake CPD, first, because it contributes to staff keeping their skills, knowledge and experience up to date. Secondly, many employers like staff to take responsibility for their own development and CPD provides the envelope in which a diverse range of development strands may be held together and leveraged for maximum benefit. Thirdly, CPD helps with succession planning. For some organisations in highly competitive sectors, CPD is a means of retaining staff. Staff vote with their feet – if the organisation is not committed to their professional development, they go elsewhere.

The benefits of CPD for colleges and universities

Colleges and universities need to ensure that the content of their courses is relevant to the needs of their students while they are studying and also as they are planning their future careers. This is particularly pressing when the students are part-time and have an agenda of concerns and challenges at work that they would like help in addressing. Discussion of CPD in tutorials or learning sets established for this purpose is a powerful way of linking this individual work-based agenda to the curriculum of the course. In recent years professional bodies such as the Chartered Institute of Personnel and Development (CIPD) have begun to lay a requirement on colleges to address CPD as a core part of the curriculum.

The benefits of CPD for the CIPD

The CIPD has a double agenda. First, as a professional body it has made clear that it expects all its members to complete a CPD plan and record at least annually. It sets this expectation because this will mean that its members keep themselves learning and therefore able to deliver more effectively than those outside the membership who do not have the push to keep up with their CPD. It will mean that the qualification will be worth more as a differentiator. In some professions – eg medicine (Sankar, 2003) – the backlash against compulsion highlights the limits to the exercise of power by professional bodies.

Secondly, the CIPD has a specific interest as a Chartered body in that it makes undertakings to the Privy Council in Britain that its members will meet certain standards in order to be able to claim their Charter status. These undertakings centre on members committing to CPD. Some branches of the CIPD, notably in Devon and Cornwall, have recognised that CPD is their core responsibility.

KEY PRINCIPLES OF CPD

Professional standards are important to every employee. We are going to use the CIPD's description of the key principles of CPD to explore why it is so important to us, as professionals.

The CIPD's key principles of CPD are:

- professional development is a continuous process that applies throughout a practitioner's working life
- individuals are responsible for controlling and managing their own development
- individuals should decide for themselves their learning needs and how to fulfil them
- learning targets should be clearly articulated and should reflect the needs of employers and clients as well as the practitioner's individual goals
- learning is most effective when it is acknowledged as an integral part of all work activity rather than an additional burden.

We shall explore each of these principles briefly here and then focus on them again, in detail, in subsequent chapters.

Professional development is a continuous process that applies throughout a practitioner's working life

It is no longer possible to do all your learning at the start of your career and then spend the rest of your working life using what you have learned. The sell-by date for professional learning is getting shorter and shorter. Our assets do not remain the same if we do not freshen them – they dwindle, and they dwindle fast.

We also live in an information age when technology is producing continual changes. We need to assess continually how these changes could help us to carry out our roles better.

Do you want to spend all your working life focused on one career or do you want to change? One developer watched his father catch the same commuter train to the same job for years and felt saddened when his father died the year after his retirement. He made a commitment to himself that he would do things differently. At the age of 30 he left a lucrative job in credit finance and retrained as an outdoor management development consultant. He is now his own boss, earns less but loves what he is doing, and no two days are ever the same.

Individuals are responsible for controlling and managing their own development

We can get what we want, if we let ourselves. Sometimes it is hard to give priority to our own needs. If we have been conditioned not to take risks or 'put our head above the parapet', it can seem difficult to plan to do so.

Our greatest limitation is the constraint of our imagination. We tend to imagine and crave for experiences that are already known by ourselves or others – more of … this, or greater than … that, or sometimes less of … the other. We frequently do not consider going beyond, experimenting with new ways of being and doing, creating a unique path.

CPD reminds us of the need not only to dream our future but also to take active steps to create our dream in reality. There's no point in standing around the photocopier, discussing, with envy, someone else's promotion. We owe it to ourselves to create such opportunities for ourselves – apply for our ideal job, sign up for that part-time course, volunteer to take on new tasks to develop our skills.

Individuals should decide for themselves their learning needs and how to fulfil them

The path we walk is unique. Colleagues, family and friends may walk alongside us for some of the way but they cannot live life for us. So many people are in careers that were shaped by schooling and family rather than being their own choice. We also know that typically an individual may experience a range of careers in their working lifetime. A professional chooses their work and their employer, sometimes consciously, sometimes unconsciously and can change – if they want to. Exploring CPD assists us both to be aware that we are making choices and to appreciate the range of options that are available.

Our CPD is not a 'puzzle' or 'jigsaw' where there is one right answer or way for the pieces to fit together. There are infinite possibilities and we need to take time to explore the range of options. The process of CPD is a little like standing at a crossroads with lots of roads radiating from the centre. We may want to wander up each of these roads a little way to see what each possible option has to offer. This can take some time and reflection but it helps us to appreciate the rich range of opportunities open to us.

Parts 2 and 3 of this book are structured in a way that will help you to explore the range of CPD options available to you.

Learning targets should be clearly articulated and should reflect the needs of employers and clients as well as the practitioner's individual goals

Charles Handy (1994: 71–3) talks about portfolio careers. Even if we have only one source of paid employment, we still need to think in a portfolio way – developing 'our own portfolio of knowledge, skills and experience' which are transferable to any new opportunity.

There are a number of perspectives on this. First, you can see yourself as developing value to employers. Second, you can develop your life purpose and mission. The distinction between these two can be somewhat illusory – especially if you start from life purpose – as people who follow their dream tend to add value wherever they go.

Third, you could see yourself as being on a journey with several attractive stopping places (employers or clients) where you stay for a while and then move on. You may or may not be clear about your final destination – what is important is the feeling of moving forward and developing.

Fourth, CPD may not involve us in doing anything different – instead it may help us to view what we do in a different way. David, when he was working in a management position he was not enjoying, came to see himself not as working in the organisation but as working on the organisation. This involved a subtle change of perspective to one that enabled him to feel more empowered.

Part 2 of this book will also assist you to seek your purpose, clarify your perspective and set clear goals to realise your future.

Learning is most effective when it is acknowledged as an integral part of all work activity rather than an additional burden

When we were working with Commercial & General Union (Gibb and Megginson, 1999), our clients and participants summarised their reasons for participating in CPD. These are described in the following box.

CONTINUING PROFESSIONAL DEVELOPMENT IN CGU

For the individual

- I will be listened to and given a fair chance to develop
- I like the idea of a detailed review of my development
- I like the balance – what I am good at and what I need to improve
- I think that a specific action plan will help me to focus.

For managers

- development needs plus action = improvements in performance
- more effective people = fewer problems for me
- I like the idea of concentrating more on learning from work experience
- it is satisfying to help people to develop.

For CGU as an organisation

- it emphasises development as a priority – not just a tag-on to other processes
- it contributes to growing a learning organisation and a good learning climate
- it grows skills of flexibility and self-responsibility
- it helps learning how to learn.

For individuals, learning is the path to a more fulfilling career and a more exciting life. For organisations it is the means of supporting staff in their development and keeping fresh their knowledge, skill and engagement with work.

GIVING PRIORITY TO CPD

Having recognised the need for CPD, how do we make time in our busy lives to do it?

This section will explore how we can increase our motivation to make CPD a priority in our working day and will also examine the loss of potential in not developing ourselves.

Professional performance = ability x motivation

Getting things done in the right way at the right time depends not only on our ability to do something but also on how much we want to do it – the effort we put into it.

One way to approach your professional development is to see it as an add-on – something separate from your work, something to do when you have a spare moment, a reward or bonus when you have finished other things.

If you are tempted to approach CPD in this way, it could be important to examine the elements of your professional performance. We are not focusing here on the skills and knowledge you possess to do your job but the ways in which you are stimulated to want to begin, follow through and complete the tasks involved.

Motivation theorists help us to be aware that we are rarely actuated just by money. We need money to furnish our basic needs for food, warmth and safety but what keeps us in a particular job are often motives like responsibility, recognition, opportunity for advancement or development and working with others.

As CPD helps us to fulfil these motives, it is central to our everyday work.

What happens if we do not make CPD a priority?

Perhaps we think that it is 'too hard' or that 'people like me don't get high-profile jobs' or that 'I wouldn't want to do better than … my friends, my partner'. We carry most of our limitations in our own heads. If we spend a few moments reflecting on those, then consider the time and effort these limitations are costing us, we may feel motivated to do things differently.

We asked a wide range of people why they do not engage in conscious and deliberate CPD, and included their responses in the following questionnaire.

Questionnaire

The exercise below invites you to take a few minutes to consider ways in which you might be unconsciously hindering your CPD.

We list a range of issues that have 'tripped up' other people and invite you to consider your own limitations and add them to the list.

WAYS IN WHICH YOU MIGHT BE UNCONSCIOUSLY HINDERING YOUR CPD

Is this a problem for you
- often?
- sometimes?
- never?

1   Not developing skills you need, like using computer programs and equipment, that could help.

2   Being fuzzy and lacking clear vision and focus.

3   Negative self-talk – eg 'It's too hard', 'I'll never …', 'I'm not the kind of person who …'.

4   Putting other people's priorities before your own.

---

5   Not confronting difficult challenges, prevaricating, avoiding issues.

6   Working to someone else's definition of success, rather than developing your own.

7   Projecting blame on to others, rather than accepting responsibility.

8   Focusing on the past instead of living in the present.

Add your own limitations below:

9

10

TRANSFORMING LIMITATIONS TO CPD

We now include a range of suggestions, linked to each of the eight points in the questionnaire, to start you thinking about transforming these limitations. These issues will be explored further in subsequent chapters.

1 Sorting out skills deficits

Book that course or find someone to work alongside you and teach you. Alternatively, delegate to someone who has the skills.

2 Fixing fuzziness

This book will help you clarify your professional direction and goals. The following metaphor and story (www.sandrastewart1@aol.com) will start you on this process and subsequent chapters will offer a range of other frameworks. Read the story and then apply it to your own life.

BIG ROCKS

One day, an expert in time management was running a seminar for very busy professionals.

He challenged them to a quiz.

He set a one-gallon wide-mouthed jar on the table in front of him. Then he produced about a dozen fist-sized rocks and put them into the jar. When the rocks reached to the top and no more could be put inside, he asked, 'Is the jar full?'

Everyone in the class said, 'Yes.'

'Really?' he replied, reaching under the table for a bucket of gravel. Then he dumped some gravel in and shook the jar causing the pieces to work themselves down into the space between the big rocks.

Then he asked the group once more. 'Is the jar full?' By this time the group were on to him. 'Probably not,' one of them responded. 'Good,' he replied. He then reached under the table and brought out a bucket of sand and sprinkled this in the space between the rocks and the gravel.

Once again he asked the question, 'Is the jar full?' 'No!' everyone shouted. Once again he replied 'Good.'

Then he took a pitcher of water and began to pour it until the jar was filled to the brim. He asked the group, 'What was the point of this illustration?'

One eager person commented, 'The point is that no matter how full your schedule, you can always fit some more things in.'

'No,' said the expert. 'Think about the order I put the things into the jar. If you don't put the big rocks in first, you'll never get them in at all.'

'What are the "big rocks" in your life?' he continued. 'Take a few moments now to make a list of them: … your loved ones … your education … your dreams … a worthy cause … mentoring others … doing things you love … time for yourself … friends … Start a list now and add to it in the next few days.'

He summarised: 'Remember to put those *big rocks* in first or you'll never get them in at all. If you sweat the little stuff [the gravel and the sand], then you'll fill your life with little things to worry about that don't really matter, and you'll never have the real quality time you need to spend on the important things [the *big rocks*].'

Activity

IDENTIFYING THE *BIG ROCKS* IN YOUR LIFE

Read the story of *'Big rocks'* again. Identify the *big rocks* in your life.

1

2

3

4

5

6

7

8

9

10

> Clarifying our *big rocks* helps us to focus beyond the minutiae of day-to-day living.

Exercises in Chapters 4, 5 and 6 offer help in implementing these priorities.

3 Choosing your attitude

Our attitude towards life has a great impact on our professional progress. Henry Ford emphasised this when he said:

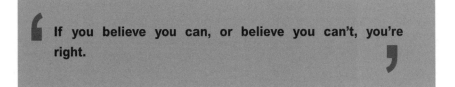

If you believe you can, or believe you can't, you're right.

Our vivid imaginations can dream up many reasons for not doing things – if we let them. It is important to recognise that in many cases these reasons are not tangible or inevitable. We can change through choosing our attitude. Attitudes are learned and can be changed over time.

4 Putting our priorities first

Managers often want us to work towards the priorities of the organisation. Increasingly people are changing jobs and career several times during their years of employment. So we have also to take responsibility for our own development and consider the span of our professional career.

For some people this feels counter-cultural – their upbringing or religion has encouraged them to put others first.

Our belief is that everyone can change and grow and that they have a responsibility to develop that potential within them. Often, when we do this, we shall have more skills to be of greater assistance to others.

5 Preventing procrastination

Preventing procrastination requires reflection, clarity of purpose, commitment and courage.

We have encountered some very elegant forms of procrastination during our discussions with people when exploring their CPD. If you find yourself procrastinating about something, reflect on the following questions:

- Does this need to be done?
- Is there a different way of doing this?
- How will this help me/others?

■　What do I need to do to increase my commitment to this project?

6　Succeeding for self

Why do we do what we do?

■　Because it excites us?

■　Because it is what is expected of us?

■　Because it is the most recent opportunity that has presented itself?

■　Because it offers job security and a reliable income?

One of the things we need to check out when we are planning our own professional development is that we are working to our own agenda and that we are doing what we want to do.

Activity

ASSESS WHETHER YOU ARE WORKING TO ACHIEVE SOMEONE ELSE'S DEFINITION OF SUCCESS

Western society equates success with achieving more, with reliability, with predictability, but for some people it may be about doing less, being more spontaneous and seeking synchronicity.

Explore your own view of success by completing the following:

My boss will consider that I am successful when I ....

....

My family/friends will consider that I am a successful when I ....

....

I shall consider I am successful when I ....

....

In order to achieve this, I need to ....

....

Frank was puzzling over his next career move. He explained that everyone from his South Yorkshire village either went down the mines or went into the army. He had done his stint in the army, was studying for a professional qualification but was confused about his future plans. In our discussions we recognised that part of his discomfort lay in the fact that he had gone beyond the expectations of his parents and his place of birth. He had become a different kind of person. He had become the kind of person who enjoyed working with and developing disadvantaged adults and he began to seek jobs that would offer him the opportunity to do this.

7 Acknowledging our responsibility

Projection is a defence mechanism that stimulates us to deflect ideas or feelings that we feel are too difficult or painful on to others.

If we find ourselves criticising others in relation to their professional progress it is useful to remember that when we point a finger at others, there are three fingers pointing back to us.

8 Living in the present

We get what we focus on.

In a meeting, one person was very stressed and kept diverting the topic from the one on the agenda to different issues. However, decisions about these issues had been made by the power-holders the previous year. No one in the meeting could influence these decisions in the present or the future. It was difficult for others in the meeting to steer the topic back to the subject on the agenda and make progress about current issues.

How often do we, or our colleagues, hold on to issues in the past which have, in our view, been unsatisfactorily resolved, rather than letting go of these so that we can give full attention to the present? If our time is spent on regrets and we are focused on the past, we have less attention and energy to explore our future development and to ask 'What can I do today that will enhance my future career?' Solutions-focused approaches to development help us to get away from a deficit-oriented approach to the past and are increasingly used in coaching (Berg and Szabó, 2005) and in change management (Jackson and McKergow, 2002). How might they help with CPD?

THE RELEVANCE OF CPD

The priority that we give to any issue depends on how relevant that subject is to us. The following questionnaire will assist you to assess the current relevance of CPD for you.

Questionnaire

Consider the extent to which the following are salient for you. Rate them on a 0–4 scale in which

4 = highly relevant

3 = somewhat relevant

2 = interesting but not relevant

1 = of not much relevance

0 = definitely not relevant to me

The reason CPD is relevant for me		Rating (0–4)
1	CPD will help me develop my career into other jobs and widen my skills and experience.	
2	CPD will assist me to look at the whole of my life, assess my work–life balance and ensure that I am not becoming complacent.	
3	I want to do CPD to help me improve my performance in my current job.	
4	It is a requirement for me to complete CPD at work.	
5	It is required that I carry out CPD as part of my assessment on a course.	
6	It is an expectation for me to carry out CPD on my course.	
7	The CIPD requires me to complete CPD.	

Note your overall score and see whether it is near to the overall maximum (28) or much lower. If it is low, note whether your score is mainly in response to the inner-directed reasons (1–3) or the external requirements (4–7). If you have a reasonable score for at least one of the inner reasons, you are likely to be able to use the suggestions in this book to pursue your self-chosen agenda.

Rothwell and Arnold, 2005, in their study of CPD by CIPD members, conclude that there are six motivations for undertaking CPD:

1   to avoid losing one's licence to practise

2   because it is enjoyable in itself

3   to make up lost ground

4   to maintain one's current position

5   to get ahead of the competition

6   to affirm one's identity as a good professional.

Which of these six do you think were confirmed by their research as being salient for FCIPD and MCIPD members in Nottinghamshire and Derbyshire? How do these motives compare with the other lists we have given in this chapter? The answer to the first question is Item 6, and to a lesser extent, Items 4 and 5. What are the implications of this for your own CPD and for organisations and the CIPD in encouraging CPD?

CONCLUSION

If we choose to give CPD priority in our lives, it can facilitate:

■   advancement and promotion

- balance and quality of life
- capability enhancement.

We have observed (Gibb and Megginson, 1999) that people who embrace CPD appear to be more engaged, less stressed, more interested in new opportunities and open to working with new colleagues.

CPD can bring excitement and change into a previously routine pattern. It can add extra meaning to staff appraisal or review, and can encourage training and development.

2,500 years ago the philosopher Heraclitus said:

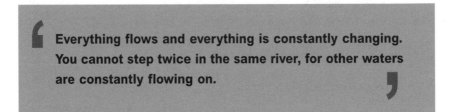

Everything flows and everything is constantly changing. You cannot step twice in the same river, for other waters are constantly flowing on.

We need to recognise that CPD is a natural process – we are always changing and growing. This book will assist you to 'go with the flow' and provide structure and ideas to make CPD feel exciting and easy.

REFERENCES

BERG, I.K. and SZABO, P. (2005) *Brief coaching for lasting solutions*. New York: W.W. Norton.

GIBB, S. and MEGGINSON, D. (1999) Employee development in Commercial & General Union. In: REDMAN, T. and WILKINSON, A. (eds). *Contemporary human resource management: text and cases*. Harlow: Financial Times/ Prentice Hall.

HANDY, C. (1994) *The empty raincoat: making sense of the future*. London: Hutchinson.

INCOMES DATA SERVICES (1999) *Career management*. IDS Study, No 678. London: Incomes Data Services.

INDUSTRIAL RELATIONS SERVICES (1998) *Learning strategies*. January, Issue 8. London: IRS.

JACKSON, R. and McKERGOW, M. (2002) *The solutions focus; the simple way to positive change*. London: Nicholas Brealy.

ROTHWELL, A. and ARNOLD, J. (2005) How HR professionals rate continuing professional development. *Human Resource Management Journal*. Vol 15, No 3. pp18–32.

SADLER-SMITH, E., ALLINSON C. W. and HAYES, J. (2000) Learning preferences and cognitive style: some implications for continuing professional development. *Management Learning.* Vol 31, No 2, pp239–256.

SANKAR, V. (2003) Big Brother is watching (your CPD). *British Medical Journal.*
Vol 327, No 7413, 11 October, p855.

TAMKIN, P., BARBER, L. and HIRSH, W. (1995) *Personal development plans:
case studies of practice.* Brighton: Institute for Employment Studies.

www.cipd.co.uk

www.sandrastewart1@aol.com

Understanding Continuing Professional Development

INTRODUCTION

Continuing Professional Development is a complex professional discipline and there is a maze of approaches that can be appropriate. In this chapter we explore the range of paradoxes and dilemmas that a person faces when they engage in CPD planning.

Each person's approach to CPD is different because everyone has a unique life experience. Making choices in relation to these paradoxes aids you in formulating the approach to CPD that best fits with your personality, your purpose and your life experience.

Activitists and pragmatists may argue that such in-depth analysis is not essential. However, CPD is something that we shall all be doing for at least the rest of our professional careers, so it is important to be thorough in diagnosing the approach that is most appropriate for each of us.

THE SEVEN PARADOXES WITHIN CPD

In our analysis of the issues involved in grasping the complexities of effective and in-depth CPD planning, we have identified seven dilemmas or paradoxes. These are:

1   compulsion or voluntarism

2   employer or individual responsibility

3   teaching or learning

4   personal development or organisational learning

5   life purpose or life experience

6   values-driven or pragmatic development

7   journey or exploration.

Where do you stand on these issues?

The questionnaire that follows is designed to help you explore each of the riddles and think about your stance on the seven paradoxes that we shall discuss in this chapter.

It encourages you either to accept the paradoxical nature of the subject or to express your clear commitment on certain issues. When you have completed and scored the questionnaire you will be in a position to say where you stand on some of the most crucial and demanding issues about CPD.

Questionnaire

For each question you have a nine-point scale upon which you can score your view. Select:

- 1 or 9 if you strongly advocate one end of the spectrum rather than the other

- 2 or 8 if you clearly advocate one end or the other

- 3 or 7 if you mildly advocate the one end or the other

- 4 or 6 if you have a 'both/and' position on the question, and see both options as more or less equally valid

- 5 if you are committed equally to both.

Issue in CPD	1	2	3	4	5	6	7	8	9	Issue in CPD
CPD is so important that everyone must be obliged to do it										CPD works only if individuals decide to commit to it voluntarily
Organisations must take responsibility for developing and managing CPD initiatives										The responsibility for CPD rests with the individual employee
Offering some clear options for short courses to meet CPD requirements helps										CPD works if individuals use a range of methods of their own choosing
CPD is about individuals learning and developing for themselves										CPD is about increasing the capacity of the organisation to learn and grow
Starting from reflecting on life purpose is a way of deepening the effects of CPD										Reflecting on what has led you to be the way you are is the best starting point for CPD

Articulating values is a way of deciding what needs to be developed in CPD									It is helpful to keep CPD grounded in what will be useful
It is important to know where you are headed when you start CPD									It is important to find new avenues to explore when undertaking CPD

Using your results

Your results will help you to decide your response to the detailed explanation of each paradox outlined below.

This questionnaire may also help you to clarify your organisation's approach to CPD. Can you gauge its possible response to your engaging in CPD planning? For example, is it likely that you will have time within your working day to implement aspects of your CPD plan?

If you are currently a full-time student and will be seeking a job at the end of your course, the results could help you to begin to define the kind of organisation that you would like to work for. Also, debate about these issues can help students to shape their assignments.

The results will also assist you to have an overview of the CPD debate so that you can develop your CPD plan within the context of that debate.

THE PARADOXES EXPLORED

Compulsion or voluntarism

In our book on self-development (Megginson and Whitaker, 1996: 46) we suggest that voluntarism has motivational advantages, but that sometimes people need a prod to get themselves going.

A resolution of this dilemma is to suggest that you do not have to follow the organisation's CPD scheme in detail, but that doing nothing about your CPD is not an option.

A particular aspect of this issue is the role of the CIPD in promoting CPD to its members. Should CPD be a requirement for those undertaking professional education? Should it be assessed? If your CPD plan were assessed by the CIPD, would that change the nature of the contents of your plan?

Then there are questions raised by the CIPD's Charter – do Charter members have to complete regular CPD records? A very strong requirement might be that the professional body should require all members to do CPD each year. Or do you think that CPD is best furthered in the profession by encouragement to engage with a voluntary process? What do you think of the view that all CIPD members sign up to CPD as part of the Code of Professional Conduct?

Employer or individual responsibility

There is a case for all employers taking on responsibility to support and resource CPD. It can be argued that it is part of the new psychological contract between employee and employer (Herriot, 1995).

On the other hand, if the company takes it over, this can reduce ownership by the individual and will also tend to direct the focus of the development towards company specific goals.

This can be useful for individuals as well as organisations, but it can also lose the passion with which a personally-chosen goal is pursued, and it will tend to narrow the range of outcomes considered.

Ecology demonstrates that monocultures – including skill monocultures – are not healthy communities and are prone to sudden collapse if the environment changes. So diversity, it could be argued, is crucial in development.

Teaching or learning

It is easy to list the kind of training courses that people undertake as part of their development. Some research commissioned by the Thames Valley branch of the CIPD into the career development of senior women in HR found that the following courses were the most frequently cited by the 20 respondents:

- 18 presentation skills
- 13 teambuilding
- 11 negotiations
- 11 communications
- 10 assertiveness
- 5 confidence-building
- 5 conflict-handling.

However, these courses were not considered the most useful sort of experience, even in the narrow area of developing skill. The same survey found that the development that had been most influential in their career had been a course only in 11 cases, of which:

- five were higher degrees
- two were CIPD professional qualifications
- two were personal development programmes
- one was a first degree

- one was with a personal coach.

So this evidence confirms much that has been reported by Mumford (1997), Revans (1998) and others, that training courses are not often significantly life-changing, even if lengthier taught programmes may be.

These results suggest that longer academic programmes (with a focus on self-development) and development through work experience were the most influential factors in this group's CPD.

Personal development or organisational learning

It is possible to treat CPD as an isolated task, separate from the rest of our lives, and a task that just has to be done. This perspective is sometimes associated with an organisational view of learning – that what I learn at and for work has no relevance to any other aspect of my life.

If we adopt this view of CPD, its effects may be limited. But even with this approach, it is possible that our lives' inherent interconnectedness will draw us into change and development that we did not expect.

This alternative view suggests that our CPD activity will ramify into all aspects of our lives, will have a range of unexpected benefits and will present challenges that we did not anticipate when we set out. Self-development needs to come with a health warning (Megginson and Pedler, 1992: 7): 'This stuff can change your life.'

In exploring learning we also need to consider who shares the responsibility for developing your organisation or your part of the larger organisation. Reg Revans (1998) pointed out that:

> **If organisations don't learn faster than the rate of change in their environment, they die.**

Is the development of your organisation addressed adequately by other means, or do you need to consider this in conjunction with your CPD?

Life purpose or life experience

Do we begin our CPD from the position that we have a life purpose towards which we are progressing, even if we are not yet clear what it might be?

Or do we adopt the view that circumstances dictate the direction that our lives will take? Our parents, our education, our communities lead us down certain paths and we find ourselves driven by nature or nurture to be what we are.

The first view of being pulled by purpose is sometimes called 'teleology' (Hillman, 1996), whereas the latter view is called 'causality'. It is interesting to speculate what difference holding one view or the other might make to your approach to your development.

Values-driven or pragmatic development

What are the effects of starting your CPD from a consideration of your values? Does it help ground how we develop on some firm and relatively unchanging principles?

Or is it more expedient and likely to yield more tangible results if we focus on whatever are the current issues in our organisation – that we work with the flow rather than run the risk of standing against it on a matter of principle?

One resolution of this dilemma is that CPD can encourage continuing Model II learning (Argyris, 1991) – changing the rules, rather than adhering to specifications. If we work in a Model II way, then instead of merely trying to improve on what exists we look for alternative ways of working that can increase effectiveness.

People operating from their values may seek new opportunities for achieving congruence between their espoused values and the way they implement those values in practical day-to-day tasks.

Consideration of this paradox will ensure that whether we operate by value or pragmatically, it will be an issue of personal conscious choice. We can do either, and do it knowingly and deliberately.

Journey or exploration

There are related but distinctive metaphors often used in describing development. One is that of the journey – where there is a destination and the challenge is to make one's way towards it; enjoying and relishing it, perhaps, but mainly focusing on how good it will be when you get there.

The other is that of exploration. Explorations, like journeys, involve going somewhere, but they differ in that we do not know where we shall end up. Goals for explorations are necessarily looser, wider, harder to define. It depends what turns up and what we discover as to what we ultimately might get out of it.

Do you think of your development as a journey or an exploration? What are the consequences of your response to this question? Journeys relate easily to the conventional apparatus of CPD – you can set goals in advance and work towards them, monitoring your achievements along the way. You have pre-defined outcomes by which you can evaluate your success. A risk is that the aspirations are narrow and may become increasingly anachronistic as things change around you. What made sense when you started can be pursued now only by ignoring what the world, the environment in which you are working, is telling you.

Another analogy is the difference between the map and the territory. When we look at a map, we know that it is a mere representation – that it is not in itself what it depicts.

It is a chart that helps us navigate in the real world – the territory we are making our way across. But is it so different when we are confronted with the territory itself?

We think when looking out over the territory that we have reality before us, but – as anyone knows who has tried to navigate on foot across open country – it is not that simple. We have a limited viewpoint, we see the context only from our own perspective, and we are often deluded in our beliefs about where we are and how what we see in front of us fits with the wider picture. Sometimes our beliefs about what we see are just plain wrong: 'I am sure that if we turn left here it will lead us to where we want to go.'

So the territory is not categorically different from the map. In both cases our perceptions mediate the experience of things as they are. Our view of both the map and the territory is just a mental model (Senge, 1990) of the world, that we use for particular purposes.

Maps, as with our view of reality, have functions other than showing what the world is like. They also motivate, orientate, give us hope, and help us to engage in collective action (Weick, 1995, p54).

CONCLUSION – DEVELOPING A HIGH LEVEL OF CURIOSITY

The central purpose of this chapter has been to examine the complexities of CPD in depth. It has provided the opportunity to explore the key paradoxes within CPD and has invited you to take a stance in relation to these paradoxes.

Some of you may not want to make choices yet. You may need to hold in awareness the conflicting nature of the paradoxes as you progress through the book and work on more pragmatic analytical exercises.

This chapter has raised many questions. You will have the opportunity to crystallise your own answers to these questions as you continue to work through Parts 2 and 3 of the book.

Another aim of this debate has been to highlight the importance of developing a high level of curiosity. In our busy day-to-day lives we often reach for the most obvious or the most immediate solution rather than examining a concept in depth.

If we are to be proficient and professional in our CPD, we need to develop a high level of curiosity so that we make time to analyse and question fundamental issues.

REFERENCES

ARGYRIS, C. (1991) Teaching smart people how to learn. *Harvard Business Review.* Vol 69, No 3, May-June. pp99–109.

HERRIOT, P. (1995) The management of careers. In: TYSON, S. (ed). *Strategic prospects for human resource management.* London: Institute of Personnel and Development. pp184–205.

HILLMAN, J. (1996) *The soul's code: in search of character and calling.* London: Bantam.

MEGGINSON, D. (1996) Planned and emergent learning: consequences for development. *Management Learning.* Vol 27, No 4. pp411–428.

MEGGINSON, D. and PEDLER, M. (1992) *Self-development: a facilitator's guide.* Maidenhead: McGraw-Hill.

MUMFORD, A. (1997) *Management development: strategies for action.* 3rd ed. London: Institute of Personnel and Development.

REVANS, R.R. (1998) *ABC of action learning.* London: Lemos and Crane.

SENGE, P. (1990) The leader's new work: building learning organizations. *Sloan Management Review.* Vol 32, No 1. pp7–23.

WEICK, K.E. (1995) *Sensemaking in organizations.* Thousand Oaks, CA: Sage.

Engaging in Continuing Professional Development

This section of the book builds on the understanding of the context of CPD you gained in Part 1 and assists you in applying the principles of CPD to your own professional practice.

The next four chapters take you through one cycle of conducting CPD. Chapter 3 focuses on self-assessment and offers a detailed framework for reflection on your current professional practice. Chapter 4 takes this work forward into planning and prioritising how you would like to develop your professional practice in the future. Chapter 5 addresses implementation, identifying the activities that you might undertake and how you can derive the learning from them. Chapter 6 looks at how you review your development and what you might do during and at the end of a CPD cycle to record and evaluate your learning.

As you work through these chapters you progress round a development spiral from where you are now to where you want to be, to how you will get there, and to looking back and seeing how you have done. See Figure 1.

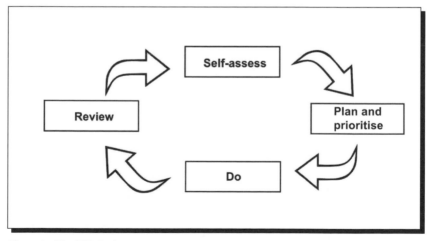

Figure 1   *The CPD Cycle*

In Part 3, Chapter 7 will help you to recognise and consolidate your CPD successes. Chapter 8 provides a range of ways for you to increase your networks. Chapter 9 introduces new methods of analysis and planning, for your next cycle of CPD.

Identifying development needs

INTRODUCTION

The first step in manifesting our future professional development is ironically not about taking action but rather about making time and space to reflect and make sense of our development to date. This chapter introduces a comprehensive framework for this process.

DEVELOPING AN 'EXTRAORDINARILY REALISTIC SELF-IMAGE'

In order for us to identify where we want to put energy into our own development, it is necessary to develop what Inglis (1994) calls an 'extraordinarily realistic self-image' (ERSI). You need this so that you can be sure that your dreams, goals and plans are built on a sound foundation: so that you know where you are at the start of your journey.

Then you can consider how you would like things to be in the future. The outputs of this consideration of where you stand now will be your development needs to be addressed in the forthcoming round of CPD.

SOURCES OF A SENSE OF SELF

To gather data to create our ERSI we need to explore six different sources:

- work itself
- reflection by self
- feedback from others
- individual psychometric and self-diagnostic measures
- organisational metrics
- professional metrics – the CPD scanner.

Each of these six sources offers particular advantages:

- Work itself is immediate and has an urgency and cogency that encourages action. If you have a pressing problem, you will want to do something about it. If you pay attention to a stretch target that you may not achieve, this strengthens the impulse to act.

- Reflection is, in our view, the crucial skill required for CPD. If you allow yourself to reflect, you will identify an agenda for development.

- Without reflection you may have lots of experiences, but you do not have the means to generalise from them and apply learning to other situations. Of course, action is also needed, but the reflection, in itself, sets an agenda and creates a situation where it is hard not to learn from subsequent experience.

- Feedback from others is useful in that it puts a check on our capacity for self-delusion. Of course, we may not agree with all the feedback we receive and the hidden or explicit injunctions within it. However, seeking out the views of others will always provide us with 'food for thought'. Even if we doubt the goodwill of someone feeding back, we can still ask, 'Why did they choose that particular bit of biased, unfair feedback to give us?' In this way we can learn from even malicious and incompetent sources of information.

- A more dispassionate source of feedback is the array of psychometrics and other self-diagnostic questionnaires about our nature, interests or preferences. These vary from professionally designed psychometric tests to informal questionnaires of the type found in the Sunday newspapers and popular management texts (including this one). These measures can give us a sense of ourselves that can be compared with others and can lead to self-insight and to understanding others.

- Organisational metrics set a business agenda for our development. Functional or leadership competencies are an attempt to influence us by our employers. They invite us to consider how we work and to nudge us towards a view of working that accords with their strategic direction. Of course, principled dissent is always possible, but it is both prudent and stimulating to consider what the avowed direction of our organisation is and to benchmark ourselves against this direction.

- Professional metrics such as the CIPD's curriculum offer a framework that can extend beyond what are often the relatively narrow confines of a job in a particular organisation. They remind us that there is more to our chosen profession than our current competencies and preoccupations.

These sources are explored in more detail in the following framework.

FRAMEWORK FOR DEVELOPING AN ERSI

The following matrix (Figure 2) assists in identifying the range of issues involved in professional development planning.

People who have used this framework have commented:

> It helped me to recall and reconsider achievements that I had forgotten. These should have been included in my current CV.'
>
> 'I was shocked when I realised I was on a career plateau. It was only after I had done the questionnaire that I acknowledged the comfortable rut I am occupying in my current role.' 'It's time for me to change.'
>
> 'When I asked my colleagues for feedback I was delighted by their response. I hadn't realised how much they valued my contribution.

Making time in our pressured lives for self-assessment can initially feel like an additional pressure. However, it can help us to stand back and look in a holistic way at all we do and challenge us to confront complacency. It can also help us to update our professional image of ourselves and recognise our unique talents.

General	Feedback from others	Organisational metrics
	Feedback from 360-degree appraisal	Organisation goals
		Competencies
	Self-assessment metrics	Professional metrics
	Reflection	Work itself
	Personal and professional congruence	Demands of current post
Specific	Aspirations/dream	Pressing issues relating to own work targets
	Individual	Organisational

Figure 2 *Framework for developing an ERSI*

We are going to start in the bottom right quadrant (work itself) because this focuses on immediate concerns which may be priorities for our attention. Then we shall address our more personal agenda, grounded in our reflection, in the bottom left quadrant. Next we shall examine feedback from others and metrics as a reality check, in the top left quadrant. Finally we shall link our findings from these quadrants to professional and organisational standards, goals and metrics in the top right quadrant.

SPECIFIC WORK-BASED ISSUES

This section assists you to assess how much you are enjoying your current role and to explore how you see your career at the moment.

We shall begin by exploring the pinch points in our work and then how we can fizz in the stretch zone.

Pinch points at work

What are the issues that you are facing at work that cause you sleepless nights? What are the challenges that are difficult to think about because you are embarrassed about the weaknesses that they demonstrate in you? What are the opportunities that lie outside your grasp because you dare not stretch out to grasp them? If you are a full-time student, consider your last work role, or look at your work as a student on the course.

When we asked a group of CIPD students to think about these, they came up with the following list:

- not getting any feedback or guidance from my boss

- being judged about how I am performing in a temporary promotion but not getting a chance to show what I can do

- having such a lot of new knowledge to acquire that I do not know where to begin

- deep-entrenched hostile attitudes from some trade union representatives

- having to manage someone much older than myself who used to be more senior than me

- needing to develop personnel procedures that no one has any faith in or values.

Your issues may be quite different from these – that is a feature of the specific needs – each person's are unique to them. So the list above is not there as a guide to what might be your needs but as an encouragement to explore your own.

Activity

RECOGNISING YOUR PINCH POINTS

Spend a few minutes identifying your pinch points and list them.

Can these be easily resolved? If so, how?

Have you identified agenda items for your development that you could include in your learning log?

Identifying areas for development is not all about pain or need. It is also about how we think of our work and life, and the next section invites you to consider your views about your work and areas where you might change your thinking.

Fizzing in the stretch zone

We are not talking about taking stimulants or going to the gym here. 'Fizzing' and 'stretching' are some of the metaphors that people use to describe that naturally occurring feeling which comes when you move from doing usual activities in the established way (comfort zone) to doing either new, exciting activities or the same activities in a different way (stretch zone). Think about being in the stretch zone for a moment:

- How familiar is this feeling?
- When did you last experience it?

It is easy to slip into routines, particularly if you have been in the same job for some time. The following questionnaire and model of career metaphors will help you to clarify if you are fizzing and stretching or if you are on a comfortable career plateau.

Activity

ARE YOU ON A CAREER PLATEAU?

Consider your previous week at work, or a typical week at work, and assess how frequently these statements applied:

Score each statement on a scale from 0 to 5, in which

        5 – felt like this every day

        0 – didn't feel like this at all

1   Not looking forward to going to work

2   Not reading messages relating to your organisation's future

3   Not acknowledging and using a wide range of your skills and knowledge

---

4   Not using your networks to share ideas or to develop your thinking

5   Not valuing your own contributions

6   Not focusing on what has been achieved

7   Not leaving work with a feeling of high self-esteem.

RESULTS

All the statements were negative and so the overall aim would be to transform each of the statements to a positive in your daily life. You may want to pick one or two of these as an area for your CPD plan (eg 'Develop skill in using networks', or 'Increase self-esteem from work'). The following summary may suggest how urgently you need to give these issues priority.

If your total score was:

30–35 Urgent need to take action to change things. Consider who can assist you with your personal development – does your organisation operate a mentoring scheme?

20–30 Need to give more priority to your personal development. Do you have a regular appraisal?

10–20 Identify what you need to do differently. Would a weekly review of progress help you?

0–10 Sounds as if your work is challenging and enjoyable. How could you make your work even more fun?

Occupying a career plateau is often a 'low energy' place to be – you tend to being doing what you have done before so there are few 'highs' in your daily working life.

Some catalyst or decision may be needed to confront the accumulation of lethargy and stimulate decisive action. It may be that one day you wake up feeling so low that you simply can't envisage another year in the same job. Taking action on the results of this questionnaire may save you from getting to this point.

When we gave the questionnaire to a group of 11 CIPD part-time students on a Master's in HRM/D course, they returned the following results:

21, 15, 14, 10, 9, 9, 9, 8, 7, 7, 6.

Career metaphor

We next asked them to think up a metaphor to describe their career. In the sequence of their scores above, the metaphors they came up with were as follows:

21   A scratched record (not moving, stuck)

15   A hijacked jet

14   Coconut (good things inside but you wouldn't know)

10   A fine wine (been left to mature and ready to open)

9   Paint splat (bits off the centre are different aspects of work, and the paint dribbling down is going somewhere, but not sure where)

9   Butterfly (moved from civil engineering to HRM: where I want to be)

9   Puppy (very new and enthusiastic)

8   Starburst (moving off in new directions)

7   Waiting patiently for change

7   *57, 58, 59 Chevrolet* (Johnny Cash song about a car made of pieces)

6   Rollercoaster (takes time to start – climbing up; but then gathers pace).

Activity

IDENTIFYING A METAPHOR THAT DESCRIBES MY CAREER

Think for a moment about your own career.

What metaphor would describe it? The metaphor may be a plant, animal, film, vehicle or a place (for example, a cave or a high wire).

Note down any ideas that come to you.

The final stage of the exercise was to link the metaphors to a map of career metaphors (see Figure 3 below).

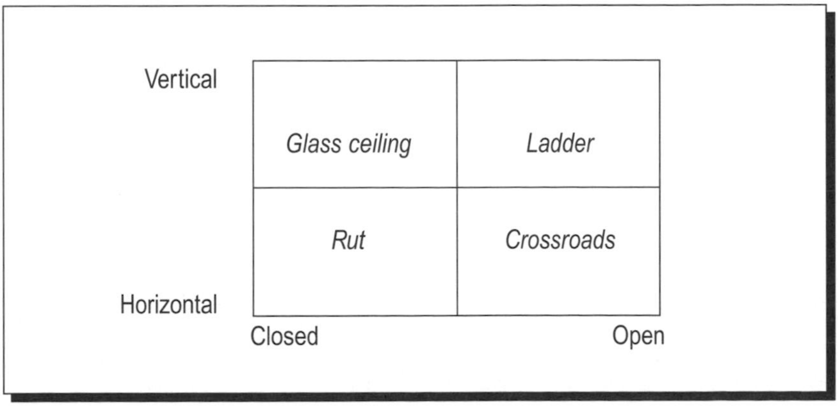

Vertical		
	Glass ceiling	*Ladder*
	Rut	*Crossroads*
Horizontal		
	Closed	Open

Figure 3 *Map of career metaphors*

Figure 3 shows that metaphors can be seen as either horizontal or vertical, and either open or closed.

Activity

IDENTIFYING YOUR CAREER WITHIN THE MAP OF CAREER METAPHORS

Which of these quadrants do you see your own career as being in at present? Are there other quadrants that appear more attractive? What do you need to do that will help you to move positions within this map?

Read the relevant questions outlined below to help you to plan to make changes.

None of the students saw their metaphor, and therefore their career, as being in the horizontal closed box (in a rut). Three saw their careers as vertical and closed. They also, not surprisingly, scored highest on the plateaued questionnaire – 21, 15, 14. Three were in the horizontal open quadrant – 7 (the Chevrolet), 8 (Starburst) and 9 (Paint splat). The remaining five saw their metaphor and their careers as open and vertical.

Here are some issues that might be particularly pertinent for people who see their careers in each of the quadrants.

Vertical closed

As you aspire to move upward and you sense that you are blocked, you could consider:

1   Do you want to move from your present organisation?

2   Can you agitate for a change in the view of your talents or your role that might open up possibilities for you?

3   Who could you network with in your organisation to explore new opportunities?

4   How can you get the credit that you deserve for the work that you have done?

Horizontal closed

This is a very contained position – not considering the move up and feeling blocked over a sideways move. One word to describe this position may be 'ravelled' – if so, what needs to happen to facilitate your unravelling? The coconut metaphor is a powerful one here:

1   Can you do anything to make your inner worth more apparent?

2   Is your rough, abrasive exterior putting people off?

3   Do you need to let go of old habits or expectations before you can consider anything new?

Vertical open

Some of the metaphors here were relatively passive (puppy; wait patiently), while others represented effort and success (rollercoaster; butterfly), so people in this quadrant can ask:

1 What am I doing to further my own development?

2 How can I spend more time doing those activities that excite me?

3 Do I want to develop through a series of highs and lows, or would a steady upward progression suit me better?

Horizontal open

People here had lots of opportunities but their ambitions may have been relatively unformed, so they could explore these questions:

1 Do I need to articulate my goals clearly and persuasively?

2 Who can help me find my direction?

3 How can I build stretch and challenge into my daily working life?

Whatever metaphor we use for our career, it provides us with additional information. For example, in another group of students, one identified 'taking the next step on the ladder' as his metaphor. This could indicate that he is dissatisfied with his current role or level and is clear about which way he wants to move. Another saw her career as a 'swamp', which indicates that she is both feeling stuck without any clear ideas or stepping stones that will assist her to move forward, and seeing progress, at best, as horizontal.

DEVELOPMENT ISSUES EMERGING FROM REFLECTION

Taking time to look in-depth at what motivates us, at how, ideally, we want to use our time, is something many of us do not programme into our busy lives.

Reflection is an opportunity to check out our personal and professional congruence. A colleague was mentoring someone and observed that what she said and what she actually did were different. He fed this information back to his mentee and she was shocked – she had not been aware of her lack of congruence. The action she took to ensure that her 'espoused values' were also her 'values in use' (Argyris, 1991) transformed her life remarkably quickly.

This process of in-depth reflection on self is similar to working with a mentor, in that it can highlight aspects of self that are hidden – the 'blind' area within the Johari window (Luft, 1984) – and makes us conscious of issues to which we have not previously given attention.

'What's stopping you from being magnificent?'

One of the finest developers we know is a consultant called Mike Humm. He built his first career as a trouble-shooter in Digital. He would be put into units of the company where things were not going well, tasked with achieving a rapid turnaround. One of his key interventions was to ask people working there, 'What's stopping you from being magnificent?' They typically had a long list of external constraints that stood in the way of their being able to perform. Mike would write down what they said and then respond, 'OK, I can sort that lot.' He would then work on the constraints that he saw come up again and again throughout the organisation.

Later he would return to the staff, one at a time, and ask, 'Now what's stopping you from being magnificent?' This time he would tend to get a shorter list and again he would go off and work on it.

The third time he went round, he did not have to say anything. The staff would forestall him. 'OK, I know what you are going to say: now it is down to me.'

Now, not all of us have got friendly Mike Humms as consultants to work on our context to liberate us to perform. This story can, however, be used in two ways in planning our own development. First, we can get a sense of the environmental constraints on our performance by imagining being asked that question.

Activity

WHAT'S STOPPING YOU FROM BEING MAGNIFICENT?

What would you say are the constraints that limit your performance, that stop you from being magnificent? List them below:

1

2

3

4

This questioning can be useful, because having identified these factors we can set goals and plans to change the things we can change and to enlist support from others to address the things that we cannot change.

We can also use the story to point us towards the question of what our performing magnificently might be like. If we have that vision clearly in our mind, then we can begin to see steps that we might take in working towards it.

Purpose and values as a starting point

If a person's development is like a journey (see the discussion in Chapter 2 about journeys or explorations, also starting from purpose or experience), then clarity about purpose and values can operate as a compass to help navigate to significant points along the way.

Sometimes when we progress through life on a seemingly programmed path we are not aware of the range of choices available to us.

During our work with professionals focusing on their development, we have found many people who are unclear about what they are here to do or what excites them. They have spent a lot of time doing what was expected of them, achieving the next thing, without questioning.

Other people have separated their personal and professional congruence – they have developed a work-self that differs from the way they are at home. They choose to do this, either consciously or unconsciously, to protect themselves from harshness in their work culture or in the tasks they have to do (making people redundant is often such a task for HR people).

Do you feel you are focused on your purpose and living your values? Victor Frankl, who survived the atrocities of concentration camps in the Second World War, reminds us that

> **Those who have a "Why" to live for can cope with any "How".**

If we know why we are doing what we do, it can help us to survive the pressures and the stresses.

Peter Cropper, first violinist with the internationally famous Lindsay String Quartet, argues that when he is playing, he is 'on purpose'. He is so inspired by the music he is engaged with that he finds this stimulating rather than depleting – he is 'fed by the music'. Can you identify a purpose and connect your work to it?

Self-actualisation or being 'on purpose'

Maslow (1943) tantalised us with the notion of 'self-actualisation' – the state at the top of his hierarchy of needs where a person is so engaged in an activity that they lose all track of time. He argued that this need was unique as compared with all the other needs in his hierarchy. Progression through his hierarchy was based on the notion that once a need was satisfied it no longer acted as a motivator. Self-actualisation was the exception to this rule – once you have experienced it you want more.

Some people discover those activities that are self-actualising at a young age; others develop them through a process of experimentation.

We have also noticed that some people are hooked by their primary needs, arrested at the base of Maslow's hierarchy, striving to achieve more and better, even though they have plenty.

Activity

ASSESSING YOUR PURPOSE AND VALUES

Consider the following questions

- Do I have a 'work-self' that is different from my 'home-self'?
- What activities do I engage in when I lose all track of time?
- Who do I aspire to be like?
- What kind of person do I want to be?
- What are my unique talents?
- What is my unique way of expressing them?
- How can I serve others?

These may be issues you have never considered before and so you may not have immediate answers to some of these questions.

One consultant we know who specialises in stimulating creativity in organisations says:

> My purpose is about challenging stodge and seriousness. I want to help people to have fun at work.

Senge's (1990) model of the leader as teacher, steward and designer, and Greenleaf's (1996) research on the servant leader may provide words or ideas that resonate for some people.

FEEDBACK FROM OTHERS

The top left quadrant of the matrix in Figure 2 focuses on feedback you have gained on your performance from colleagues close to you and from metrics.

Feedback from others is put in the general and individual quadrant because in organisations it is often given on the basis of a competency or leadership framework. The self-assessment metrics similarly have a general framework, and you are primarily interested in just your own personal score.

Gaining appropriate feedback

Do you get enough feedback from others? Organisation cultures, in our experience, differ quite markedly in the extent to which they encourage and enable feedback. In some companies feedback is a way of life. In others it is restricted to a stilted and embarrassing, once-a-year, paper-based employment ritual called the annual appraisal.

Another consideration is the balance of positive and negative feedback that we receive. Many cultures seem to be better at giving the bad news. There are some where the reverse is the case, and good news predominates. When we worked in Texaco, one HR professional said to us that:

> **The trouble was that there was so much positive supportive feedback in my department that I couldn't get a sense of how I needed to develop, of what was currently wrong.**

Appraisal

It has been said that the only company that can benefit from appraisal is one that doesn't need it! This cryptic comment means that only in companies where there is freedom from threat and people are happy to take the bulk of the responsibility for managing their learning, will appraisal be a process that enhances learning.

EFL CASE: WEEKLY APPRAISAL CONVERSATIONS

A leader whom we respect, called Frank Lord, developed a small organisation – with a turnover of £3m – into the market leader in his field with a turnover of £55m within three years.

In EFL everyone had appraisal conversations every week, and people chose whom they had them with. It could be their line boss but it could be anyone else whom the individual felt could support their development.

Data from these conversations were brought together every week by a cross-functional team, who used them to alert the executive team to the issues that needed addressing urgently.

This was a rapidly growing high-pressure business, and yet people found time to have these discussions weekly, and management found time to do something about them.

360-degree feedback

You may, as part of your normal working practice, be expected to gain feedback from all the people you work with through a formal 360-degree appraisal and feedback process.

BP EXPLORATION CASE: TRANSFORMATION FOR BOTH INDIVIDUAL MANAGERS AND FOR THE ORGANISATION CULTURE AS A RESULT OF 360-DEGREE FEEDBACK

In the early 1990s, John Brown, CEO of BPX, introduced 360-degree appraisal throughout the organisation in a top-down process. The authors both worked as facilitators during this process.

The managers we worked with at BPX were initially apprehensive before they received their feedback. However, when we analysed the detailed results most were much cheered and others rather touched by the feedback they gained. It was generally more positive and constructive than they had expected.

Some teams used humour to get their point across. One manager had received clear feedback that he was not listening enough. He admitted that this was a problem for him. In the follow-up meeting with his team, when he was planning what to put in his development plan, he stopped listening and his team burst out laughing. They had spontaneously developed an effective way of reminding him to keep focused.

Our colleagues are often kinder and more perceptive than we give them credit for. One HR professional did the previous exercises and realised that she was both on a career plateau and had been putting others' needs before her own.

She spoke to her boss and arranged a meeting to talk about doing things differently. At the start of the meeting, her boss thanked her for taking the initiative to set up the meeting. He had been concerned that she hadn't got any fresh challenges but had been hesitant to suggest ideas, as he was not sure she had fully recovered from the effects of surgery. They then discussed a range of possible options for change.

Feedback, whether it comes from a standardised framework or from our assertive asking, can give us a reality check on how we are performing. Do you need to set a goal to get more feedback? If you do, the next chapter suggests ways of doing this. Or does the feedback that you have already received suggest one or two key needs that you may have for your development? If so, note them down in your CPD log.

SELF-ASSESSMENT METRICS

In building a realistic picture of yourself, metrics can be useful. There is a vast range of these tests and inventories. We highlight a number of popular ones, and indicate how they can be helpful in CPD planning.

Personality frameworks

Personality measures such as Myers-Briggs Type Inventory® (Hirsh and Kise, 2000) or the ancient and powerful framework of the Enneagram (Palmer, 1995) can throw light on to how we operate.

Personality frameworks, however, do not present a direct agenda for change. Myers and Briggs emphasise that their 16 types represent a range of different ways to be a wonderful human being, so there is no need to change.

Additionally, it is very difficult and largely fruitless to strive to change our personality. It is laid down early in our lives and it seems to run deep, and not be very amenable to change. Better, personality theorists suggest, to come to terms with how we are and to recognise what our type can bring to our chosen work.

Personality frameworks are also valuable in helping us to understand the motives and drives of others. So any goal we set as a result of looking at our personality is likely to be about coming to terms with self or understanding others more deeply.

Belbin's Team roles

Other measures give us more scope for change. For example, Belbin's famous 'Team roles' (Belbin, 1993) are somewhat amenable to development.

If we gather feedback from others as to how they see us, we can find whether we have a coherent, a discordant or a confused profile (Belbin, 1993, p83).

In situations where the view is discordant – ie others agree among themselves but disagree with us – we need to do some work on finding out why others see us differently from the way we see ourselves.

If the view is confused, then we could look at why others cannot build an agreed picture of what we are like and how we operate in teams.

This could highlight a need to develop a clear style of contribution to a team. Belbin's earlier work (Belbin, 1981) suggested that we could not move team roles from one which we hardly used at all, but that we could increase the use of those that were in the middle range.

Activity

LEARNING ABOUT OURSELVES THROUGH THE USE OF SELF-ASSESSMENT METRICS

What metrics have you used to assist you to learn more about yourself? What suggestions for development come from your scores? How have you implemented these suggestions? What difference has this made to your professional practice?

In what ways have these tests helped you to learn more about the people you work with?

Metrics can enable us to know more about ourselves, to understand others better and to a limited extent can help us set an agenda for personal change.

ORGANISATIONAL METRICS

This is the quadrant where we assess our own needs and aspirations in terms of professional standards and organisational expectations.

Organisational goals

When organisations set up change processes, they often specify what these changes will require of individuals. These lists can be a useful benchmark for a personal development agenda. Sometimes the changes are expressed in terms of values, as in the case below.

KELLOGG'S CASE: A VALUES-DRIVEN AGENDA

Kellogg's is the world's leading producer of cereals and a leading manufacturer of convenience foods, such as cereal bars, frozen waffles, toaster pastries, cookies and crackers. In order to add coherence and direction to their efforts to develop the company, leaders in Kellogg's Europe have specified the organisation and people elements that they see as important in building high-performing teams. They suggest that the core capabilities required are:

- consumer understanding and brand development
- designing and delivering great products
- business planning and management
- customer management.

These capabilities inhere in the organisation as a whole. The next section of their specification, however, sets a personal agenda for employees. This takes the form of six value statements:

- We act with integrity and show respect
- We are all accountable
- We have the hunger and humility to learn
- We are passionate about our business, our brands and our food
- We love success
- We strive for simplicity.

The specification for the kind of people and culture that the organisation wants is likewise uncompromising:

- a strong organisation of committed, flexible and capable people who want to win as a team
- leaders who live the values and develop talent

> ■ a winning culture based upon openness, trust and recognition of performance.
>
> From our work with Kellogg's it is clear to us that people take these specifications seriously and attempt to live by them.

Activity

WHAT CAN I LEARN FROM KELLOGG'S?

What challenges would a specification like Kellogg's present for your development? Can you specify how you would need to develop to match these specifications? Are there elements in the specification that you find a stretch?

What would be your response to these challenges if you worked in Kellogg's?

If you are currently employed in an organisation:

Does your own organisation have an equivalent set of statements?

What development agenda does this create for you? Note down any key issues that are raised for your development by the goals, values, culture and core capabilities that your organisation seeks to live by.

Competencies

Many companies have sets of leadership competencies, practices or capabilities. These too can present a clear agenda for professional development.

We have selected – in this composite case study of a number of organisations we know – some of the stronger statements that we have come across. How do you react to these statements? Do they provide you with an agenda for your own development?

COMPOSITE CASE: DEMANDING LEADERSHIP COMPETENCIES

- ■ Vision – see the big picture no matter how complex
- ■ Impact and influence – find the most effective strategy for getting people's commitment and support
- ■ Drive – demonstrate passion, conviction and energy, and create an infectious hunger to deliver better performance
- ■ Focus – focus on delivering the important – dispense with the unnecessary
- ■ Provoking change – openly challenge existing ways of doing things, in the face of actual or expected threat, criticism or resistance

- Inspiration – translate corporate ambition into something that turns people on; something that means more to them as individuals

- Lead the pace – we act as catalysts, driving for results and restlessly seeking to win.

Activity

ASSESSING MYSELF AGAINST THE DEMANDING LEADERSHIP COMPETENCIES

Explore your reaction to each individual statement.

What challenges do each of them represent for you? What would it be like – what would you have to change – for you to deliver on all of them?

What do you expect would be the effect of the entire management of an organisation operating on these principles?

PROFESSIONAL STANDARDS

Another criterion against which you can judge your development is the Professional Standards of the CIPD. These are available by a link to the CIPD website, www.cipd.co.uk. Using the search facility on the site, key in 'CPD' and see what resources are offered to you. How could these be useful for diagnosis?

The invitation to users of this book is to explore the Standards and see if there are particular skills or knowledge items, or a cluster of such items, that give them a high priority area for their development. If you find such areas, then add them to the other notes that you have made in reading the first three chapters of this book, to come up with your own agenda for change.

CIPD requirements

The CIPD seeks three sets of outcomes from the Professional Development Scheme that rely substantially on CPD as well as on more academic portions of the course. These are:

- the CIPD professional as a 'thinking performer'
- the CIPD professional as a 'business partner'
- the five key BACKUP competencies.

Each of these frameworks offers a set of challenges that can be a source of an agenda for your CPD plan.

Thinking performers need to show that they possess:

- personal drive and effectiveness
- people management and leadership
- business understanding
- professional and ethical competence
- added value
- continuing learning
- analytical and intuitive/creative thinking
- customer focus
- strategic capabilities
- good interpersonal skills.

Business partners must:

- add value for the organisation
- collaborate with others inside and outside the organisation.

The key competencies in the BACKUP framework are:

- business orientation
- application capability
- knowledge of the subject matter
- understanding
- persuasion and presentation skills.

These three different takes on the requirements for full professional membership can be useful in identifying areas for CPD. For instance, if you are attending a course, you may do lots of presentations, but have you had experience of actively persuading people to adopt a course of action or a policy? If not, this could be an area for you to focus on with your CPD.

The other framework that the CIPD provides is the CPD scanner, which helps you to review the entire CIPD curriculum and to determine which are the areas where you have the greatest need. This can be particularly useful for full-time students who do not have an organisation on which to base their self-assessment.

Activity

ASSESSING YOUR THINKING PERFORMER, BUSINESS PARTNER, BACKUP AND CPD SCANNER COMPETENCIES

Look at the three frameworks above and compare them to your current skills, knowledge and experience.

Are there areas where you lack experience? If so, make a note of them.

> Think of ways in which you could use this information as a useful source for creating your CPD agenda for the future.

Senior HR professionals may have a more individual agenda (see Appendix 1 for an example) whereas Burcher et al, 2005, suggest that a focus on strategic competencies represents a way forward.

CONCLUSION – THE AGENDA FOR CHANGE

There have been a number of points in this book so far that will yield you possible areas for development in your own CPD. Ones that we particularly want to highlight are:

- Ways in which you might be hindering your CPD – see Transforming your limitations (Chapter 1)

- Assess your reasons for doing CPD – see Relevance of CPD (Chapter 1)

- Review your beliefs about CPD to embrace paradox – see The seven paradoxes within CPD (Chapter 2)

- Identify your career metaphor and decide what to do about it – see Career metaphor (Chapter 3)

- Consider questions around purpose – see Assessing your purpose and values, and What's stopping you from being magnificent? (Chapter 3)

- Use feedback you have, or seek to increase the amount you receive – see Gaining appropriate feedback (Chapter 3)

- Use Self-assessment metrics, Organisational goals or Competencies (Chapter 3)

- The use of the CPD requirements discussed immediately above (Chapter 3).

At this stage gather as many issues as arise from your reflections based upon what you have read so far. Make a summary of your list in your CPD log.

To bring this summarising activity to life we give below an example of a CPD log of someone who had worked through this book so far.

Sandy's development log

We shall follow Sandy's progress over the next three chapters, so begin here by developing a view about what you see as the issues for Sandy. At the same time, keep your own CPD log and see what the issues are for yourself.

Note that Sandy had not done all the activities, and the outcome of some of them seemed vague. However, you may be able to discern a pattern emerging. If you were Sandy, what would be the development agenda that you would create from this log, and why?

SANDY'S CPD LOG

1   Reason for doing CPD. Mainly because I am told to – more by college and the CIPD than by work.

2   Transforming limitations. I lack a clear vision and focus for my development. And I engage in a lot of negative self-talk, but that is not surprising given the lack of support I get and the threats hanging over me at work.

3   Beliefs. If I am going to make this work it is down to me. Work should help more but I can't see it happening.

4   Metaphor. It's a sort of crossroads, but there is one path going up a hill – lots of brambles growing across it.

5   Purpose. I joined Personnel to help people and I seem to spend most of my time saying no to requests. Negative culture – overall; great colleagues; distant boss.

6   Feedback. I am invisible. Low impact. Nice, but carrying messages saying no.

7   Self-assessment metrics. Myers-Briggs – INFJ. How can I use the strengths of this type?

8   Organisational goals. Cynicism about the change process. Do I believe in it?

9   CPD scanner. Huge gap in two modules not taken – Managing learning, and Organisational knowledge and change management.

10 CPD Core competencies. Not a business partner; not exercising leadership outside my own team.

If you are more senior than Sandy, you may like to refer to Appendix 1 where an example of a senior HR manager, who we call Chris, identifies needs and there is also a description of what was done about them.

In the next chapter we shall explore how to focus this list on your development agenda. We shall introduce exercises to summarise and clarify the data you have gathered and suggest ways of drawing out a manageable set of goals.

REFERENCES

ARGYRIS, C. (1991) Teaching smart people how to learn. *Harvard Business Review.* Vol 69, No 3, May-June. pp99–109.

BELBIN, R.M. (1981) *Management teams: why they succeed or fail.* London: Heinemann.

BELBIN, R.M. (1993) *Team roles at work*. Oxford: Butterworth-Heinemann.

BURCHER, P.G., LEE, G.L. and SOHAL, A.S. (2005) A cross-country comparison of careers in logistics management in Australia and Britain. *International Journal of Logistics Management*. Vol 16, No 2. pp205–217.

GREENLEAF, R.K., FRICK, D.M.(ed) and SPEARS, L.C. (ed) (1996) *On becoming a servant leader: the private writing of Robert K. Greenleaf.* San Francisco, CA: Jossey Bass.

HIRSCH.S. and KISE,J. (2000) *Introduction to type and coaching*. Palo Alto, CA: Consulting Psychologists Press.

INGLIS, S. (1994) *Making the most of action learning*. Aldershot: Gower.

LUFT, J. (1984) *Group processes: an introduction to group dynamics*. Mountain View: CA: Mayfield.

MASLOW, A. (1943) A theory of human motivation. In: BUCHANAN, D. and HUCZYNSKI, A. (1997) *Organizational behaviour: integrated readings*. Hemel Hempstead: Prentice Hall. pp45–61.

PALMER, H. (1995) *The enneagram in love and work: understanding your intimate and business relationships*. New York: HarperSanFrancisco.

SENGE, P. (1990) The leader's new work: building learning organizations. *Sloan Management Review.* Vol 32, No 1. pp7–23.

Prioritising needs and selecting appropriate activities

CHAPTER 4

INTRODUCTION

In this chapter we build on the data you compiled from assessing your current professional practice. We now move forward into planning and prioritising how you would like to develop your professional practice in the future.

We begin by exploring ways to summarise your development agenda. Then we shall engage with two contrasting diagnostic approaches – focusing on gaps or defining steps. The need for prioritising will be addressed and ways of selecting goals will be examined. Issues around what to do if you are not a planner and find prioritising difficult are highlighted. These considerations will culminate in an exploration of the format and contents that you can use to specify your CPD plan.

SUMMARISE YOUR DEVELOPMENT AGENDA

At the end of Chapter 3 we suggested that you pull together a range of activities or reflection opportunities that might have been triggered by reading the first three chapters of this book and doing the suggested activities.

We now need some criterion for deciding which of these needs (and others that you might identify) should be given priority. You need to be clear as to what the key priorities are for you in developing yourself. We suggest that this check involves you in identifying what would make you world class in all aspects of your development. This is addressed in the next section.

World class me

This process helps you to check that you have articulated and included all the important aspects of your life in your CPD. Although CPD relates primarily to your professional self, it is important to scan all aspects of self as we are holistic human beings, and how we are functioning in one area of our life directly affects performance in the others. Furthermore, our activities outside work can point to possible changes in direction that may be coming over the horizon towards us in our work.

Richard Field, a top team developer and executive coach, has created a process for exploring a 'world class me'. He has adapted it from Ishikawa's fishbone quality process. He uses it to help individuals build a powerful vision for their future and one to which they are deeply committed.

In this activity, you are asked to consider each of the areas of your life which are central to you or where you would like to make them central. We suggest that these can be both work-related and personal areas. Aim for six areas plus or minus two.

Name each of these areas and write the name at the end of one of the main bones coming out of the backbone. The example in Figure 4 shows the areas chosen by Tom, an organisation development consultant who worked in non-governmental organisations in Africa.

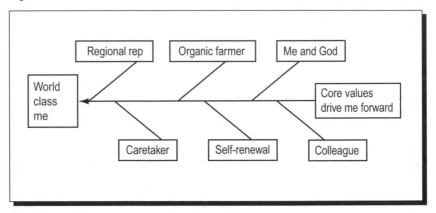

Figure 4   *Fishbone for Tom's world class me*

Then for each area in turn ask yourself the question, 'What would have to happen in order for me to be a world class me?' Then ask, 'What else?' and repeat this question until you feel emptied of all the ways in which you would manifest a world class you in that area.

Now read through the lists of what would happen to make a world class you in this area, then close your eyes, and imagine that all these have been achieved. Then say to yourself, 'Now I am a world class person. Is there anything else I need to add?' Note down anything that comes up – you are attempting to manifest all your aspirations and desires in this area.

When Tom did this for his role as 'colleague' he came up with the items shown in Figure 5.

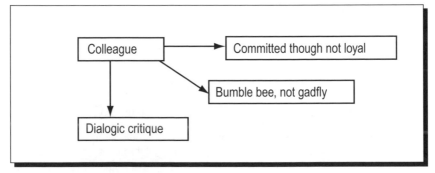

Figure 5   *Detail of areas under 'Colleague' in Tom's fishbone*

Then move on to the next big part of your life and go through the same process there. When you have completed your last area ask yourself, one more time, 'Is there anything else?' Add whatever comes up.

You now have a map of your desires for world class you. Post these somewhere prominent where you will see them every day. These aspirations will begin to work on you whether you like it or not!

However, you may want to drive the process along. In this case you can use the importance/urgency quadrants to decide where to begin work. For each of the small branches in your fishbone, ask the question, 'Is this important or unimportant; urgent or non-urgent?' You could mark each branch with two letters to indicate your view.

Richard recommends starting to make a plan with those items that are important and urgent – clear those out first, to reduce anxiety and ready yourself for a more sustainable and deeper approach to development.

Another way, following Stephen Covey (1990), would be to focus on the areas that are important and non-urgent. It is in this quadrant, Covey argues, that we make the most difference in our lives.

Activity

DRAW A FISHBONE OF YOUR WORLD CLASS ME

Draw a fishbone for working towards a world class me following the process outlined above.

What issues does this highlight for your CPD plan?

Does the fishbone format suggest a way of laying out your CPD, or do you prefer the conventional table that we discuss later in this chapter?

It can be useful to do this activity in pairs because this helps to ensure that the emptying described above occurs in each area.

How do the areas identified by this activity compare with your lists from Chapters 1–3? Does this plan for your life lead you to emphasise certain aspects of your development agenda rather than others? Use it to reduce your list to the key levers or influences for change.

Steps or gaps?

What is missing from the following set of numbers?

1 2 4 5 7 8

It is tempting to say, '3 and 6' or '0, 3, 6 and 9' or 'multiples of 3' or (as someone suggested to us recently) '13 to 44 and 46 to 77'. However, all these answers accept the premise that stands out in the question – that there is something missing. Another sort of answer would be:

> **Nothing – everything that's there is there.**

This conundrum illustrates the contrast between what we call the deficit model of CPD and the capability approach. The deficit model focuses on exploring what we lack, often referred to as the training gap. This can be contrasted with an approach that asks, 'What new steps do I want to take?' or 'What new areas do I want to get into to apply the skills that I already have?' We could call this the capability approach.

Much thinking and writing about training emphasises the training gap. Of the issues you have identified for your CPD how many of them are based upon gap psychology and how many are capability-based – about the steps you want to take? Which are the items that seem to feed your development best? Use this as a criterion for focusing on a short set of priority goals. If you know you respond well to the push of lacks and gaps, emphasise these. If you are heartened and encouraged by the pull of increased capabilities, then go for those.

To give you a sense of the difference between the two approaches, the CPD scanner referred to in Chapter 3 is a gap-based analysis, so review your experience of working through that. Compare it with the activity below, adapted from Mulligan (1999, p 141), an excellent example of the genre of books now appearing on life coaching, and a capability approach stretching towards future aspirations.

Activity

INTERVIEW YOURSELF

Imagine your ideal job: note as much detail as you can about what you would do, the sort of organisation, the kind of colleagues, the pressures and the satisfactions, the pay and conditions.

Now put yourself in the role of the HR person interviewing for the position, or if it is a self-employed job, perhaps take the role of a bank manager, considering funding the new enterprise.

Prepare an application form and a job and personal specification for the job.

Then, reverting to your role as interviewee, fill out the application form and review your capabilities against the specifications.

Now, back to the assessor role – would you give yourself the job? If yes, then you are ready to make it happen in reality. Go for it. If not, are there some stretch targets inherent in the specification that give you a lead in how to move forward?

Examine your set of draft goals and prune them according to whether you see yourself pushed by deficits/gaps or pulled by desired capabilities/steps.

BALANCED GOALS

Another way of reviewing the goals that you are accumulating is in terms of the balance across the various areas of your life. Some people will tend to focus only upon work. If you have done this deliberately and consciously, then that is fine – stay with it. However, if you have just found yourself doing this out of habit or preoccupation, then it may help to look at other areas where you might usefully consider setting goals.

We created (Megginson, 1994) a framework called SPICE, which covers a range of areas and has a memorable acronym. Setting goals in the areas of spirit, physical-self, intellect, career and emotion will, we suggest, put spice into your life.

Review your goals now and see if there are any of the areas where you need to add or subtract emphasis. To help with this process we give a few cases below that illustrate the power of goal-setting in each of these areas. They are all real cases with the names changed.

Spirit
Linda is an organiser of a national voluntary organisation involved with equal opportunities. She has a religious belief based on the traditions of her family and she has a commitment to doing good work that she feels contributes something important to society. However, beneath this smooth surface she has some doubts and questions about her own beliefs and about the life that she leads. She tries to ignore them and keep busy with her demanding job and the calls on her time from her growing family. Nonetheless she retains a need to explore more deeply questions of purpose and identity, which she sees as a spiritual quest.

Physical
A striking example of how rebalancing can have an effect on work progress is a Sheffield professional called Dan. He was a capable but introverted individual contributor in a large organisation. He decided to join a gym and enjoyed this so much that he then took up running and built his fitness and strength with a range of other activities. One thing led to another and he became more confident and outgoing when the situation required it. He joined a running group that met each Saturday morning and then had breakfast together afterwards. There were a number of business, academic and civic leaders in this group. He learned to network and has become a successful entrepreneur running a consultancy company based in Sheffield, with a branch in London. From seeing himself as a working-class lad who just sat at home in the evenings watching TV, he now has a fuller life as a mover and shaker in his city.

Intellect
Simon has had a series of routine civil service jobs and has decided to break out of them by attending a full-time Master's in HRM. In the course of this he

finds a fascination with ideas and recognises that his critical and somewhat cynical view of organisations and management can be developed into a strong critique of existing organisational practices. He changes his mind about his work direction and rather than seeking a professional job in a company, he undergoes further years of low pay and pressure from his family in the pursuit of a PhD. He obtains a job at a top university and builds a successful academic career.

Career
Aileen feels trapped in her current job in the HR department of a local authority, where she has been employed for 12 years. Her husband is unemployed and this adds to the pressure not to think about alternative careers, especially as they live in an area of high unemployment and are committed to remain there for family reasons. However, the pressure from her boss is making her ill and she feels that she is losing the skill and confidence that she built up over the years. Following some intensive sessions with a career counsellor, she decides that she has nothing to lose in looking for a secure job in neighbouring areas. This helps her in a surprising way by enabling her to feel and be more resourceful in her existing organisation.

Emotions
Cameron is an experienced company director, with a long track record of success on boards of large companies, who has also chaired fast-growing medium-sized companies through periods of rapid growth. He now works as a freelance top team consultant and non-executive director. In spite of all his success, he has a pattern of difficulty with boards he is helping. Some find him overbearing, and his desire to ensure that things he can envisage will happen leads him to interfere with the function of the executive directors he works with. He finds this hard to acknowledge. He needs courage to face it himself and courage to persist and contradict the pattern in the relationships he is involved with. He uses a mentor to help him address these issues.

Activity

SPICE GOALS

Considering the examples above, where do you place the emphasis of your goals – spirit, physical-self, intellect, career, emotions?

Is the emphasis that you currently have appropriate for your purpose and long-term goals?

If not, in which areas do you need to increase your emphasis?

Another stretching model that we like is Hawkins' (1999) BEST model. He suggests that we can set goals that get the best out of us if we look for goals that help us to:

- broaden – move us into new areas

- enjoy – get us doing more of the things that we love

- stretch – take us into new areas, doing more, facing bigger challenges

- think – challenge our understanding and mastery, demanding deeper insight or broader perspective.

GOALS AND PLANS

Why do some people love plans and others hate them? Many books on development seem to work on the assumption that everyone likes to plan and all they need is a framework that shows them how to do it then everything will be fine.

We recognise that this is not the case for everyone. Some people are planners, but others (we call them 'emergent') do not take to the planning process at all. They are inclined to say that they prefer to plunge into an activity and see what comes up. They may be active learners but they don't plan.

Are you one of these emergent learners? What should such people do? Can planners learn anything from the emergent learners? This section explores the answers to these and related questions. The frameworks outlined here are discussed more fully in Megginson (1994; 1996).

Activity

PLANNED OR EMERGENT LEARNING

Complete the questionnaire below, scoring:

> 6 = always true of you, or you totally agree
> 5 = usually true of you, or you usually agree
> 4 = often true of you, or you often agree
> 3 = sometimes true of you, or you sometimes agree
> 2 = occasionally true of you, or you occasionally agree
> 1 = seldom true of you, or you seldom agree
> 0 = never true of you, or you never agree.

1   Writing down appraisals of my work performance is an important basis for my development.

2   For me, learning is a planned process of setting goals, achieving them and setting new goals.

3   In conversation with others I often come to new understanding of what I have learned.

---

4   I regularly prepare a learning contract or CPD statement outlining my plans.

5   It is important to me to add to/change my learning plans frequently in the light of new information.

6   I set goals for my own learning.

7   In order to learn from experience I reflect frequently upon what happens to me.

8   I set targets for my development.

9   It is important to be open to experience, then learning will come.

10   I use a learning contract or CPD statement regularly to focus on my progress in developing.

11   Most of my new learning emerges unexpectedly from things that happen.

12   You can't plan significant learning.

The scores that you gave to the following items can be summed to give you totals for planned and for emergent learning strategies:

Planned questions	Emergent questions
1	3
2	5
4	7
6	9
8	11
10	12
Total planned =	Total emergent =

What are the advantages of having a combination of learning strategies of the kind indicated by your scores? What are the disadvantages?

We allocate scores into four categories, see Figure 6, which are named as follows:

Sleepers – planned less than 17; emergent less than 21.

Warriors – planned 17 or more; emergent less than 21.

Adventurers – planned less than 17; emergent 21 or more.

Sages – planned 17 or more; emergent 21 or more.

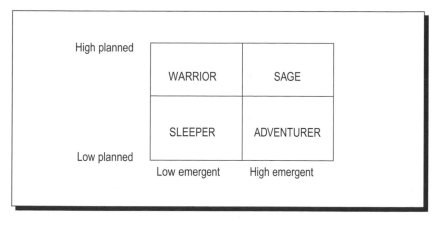

Figure 6 *Planned and emergent learning strategies*

What do we see as the implications for each of the styles? We suggest the following:

Sleepers can begin by opening up their awareness of their own lives, by reflection and by building attention and engagement – see John Jeffrey's model for creating a steady focus and intensifying our experience in Chapter 9. Any of the activities for warriors or adventurers will also help.

Warriors will be likely to find planned exercises to their liking. In our view they can deepen their learning by developing capability as emergent learners too. Learning logs and some of the reflecting on experience activities in Chapter 6 may be useful here.

Adventurers will tend to find many of the suggestions for activities in this part of the book irksome. We would argue that they would nonetheless be well advised to persist because balanced learning strategies with lots of planning in addition to their strengths as emergent learners seem to be the most effective in developing oneself.

Sages are either already impressive learners or perhaps generous self-markers. Assuming that the result is a genuine one, then the challenge for sages is first to keep up the momentum of continuing the learning they are doing already (Chapter 9 offers suggestions on how to do this). The second challenge is to help others with their learning, and to act as a role model for others.

GOAL-SETTING THEORY

Having thought through the implications of your learning strategy for approaching your CPD, the next framework to take into account is a model of adult development and its implications for goal-setting. There are many stage models of development in modern times, stretching back to Piaget. The one that we use suggests that as we develop as adults we pass through various stages or modes of being. The modes model is discussed further in Boydell and Leary (1996) and in Pedler *et al* (1997, pp 200–12).

Each mode has certain key characteristics and strengths, and the large movements of our lives, when we notice that we are viewing the world from a radically different perspective, are about moving from one mode to the next.

Figure 7 briefly describes each of the modes, which may help you to identify where you stand in your own development. This can be useful as it can pinpoint what the next major transformative step may be for you. Which mode you are operating from also has implications for your approach to goal-setting, as we shall see.

The model begins at the bottom, and as we develop we work up through the modes over the years.

The implications of the modes of development model for our CPD are:

- We can explore where we stand now in our movement through the modes and what the next major transition might be for us and how we could orientate ourselves towards it.

- We can diagnose whether we are unlikely to take to goal-setting as we do not yet have a fully functioning ego to drive us forward (modes 1–3); or whether we are likely to be comfortable with goal-setting at an individual level (modes 4 and 5); or whether we are somewhat beyond individual goal-setting and more inclined to think of the whole organisation or to live fully in the moment (modes 6 and 7).

Activity

POSITIONING YOURSELF IN THE MODES MODEL

From Figure 7, can you identify where you stand in the modes model?

Do you sense that you have just recently engaged with your current mode or are you ready to move forward? If you are just into your current mode, what kind of development activities will help you to make the most of it? Is there a dark side to your current mode; how can you guard against this becoming dominant? (See Chapter 7 – Addressing the demonic aspect.)

If you are ready to move on, what kind of development activity can help with the transition?

If you are in modes 1–3, what can you do to move towards mode 4 where goal-setting will make more sense? Are there, nonetheless, goals you can set to maximise your contribution at any of these levels?

If you are in mode 6 or 7, what can you do to help others set goals useful to them? Are there still some areas where you could benefit from setting personal goals even if it does not seem congenial?

Mode	Characteristics	Approach to goal-setting	Transition to next mode
7 Dedicating	Committed to a cause or principle, living in flow, self-actualising	Beyond goal-setting – living in the moment; very long-term intentions	
6 Connecting	Committed to community – serving others and maximising contribution of all	Collaborative approach to strategy, personal and group goals interrelated	Abandoning restraint and becoming whole-heartedly engaged at every moment
5 Experimenting	Developing deep expertise and your unique contribution	Commitment to own goals and to contribution of your function or unit	Leaving ego and 'us and them' behind and acting in the interests of the whole
4 Experiencing	Developing breadth, choosing a range of activities to extend experience	Sense of personal power and inquiry; willingness to try new things	Deciding upon your unique contribution and developing this with focus and clarity
3 Relating	Fitting in with the norms of the organisation or group; being a good citizen	Concern for fitting in means that individual goals are hard to set as this may separate you from others	Recognising that you have the power to choose and that your choices make a difference
2 Adapting	Making minor adjustments to ensure that the rules work in the practical situation	Goals set only round getting the job done according to requirements	Letting go of focus on the rules and widening your concerns to fit into the community or workgroup
1 Adhering	Obeying or following the rules, practices and routines that are established	Goals only set in terms of meeting the specification laid down	Recognising that sometimes the rules do not cover all eventualities and that practice requires flexibility

Figure 7   *Modes of development*

The activity consists of a long list of questions. Not all will apply to you, but we find that consideration of this model can lead to a deeper understanding of the benefits and difficulties involved in goal-setting.

PRIORITIES – THE FINAL CHECK

So far, we have suggested that your world class me, your self-interview, your SPICE goals, your learning strategy – planned or emergent – and your mode of development, can all help you in prioritising goals.

There is one final check that we have found useful in boiling down your goals from a long list you may have assembled to a set that is short enough to help you to focus. This final check involves asking, 'Do I need to do more of the same, or do I need to branch out?'

Phil was a self-employed trainer who was doing well and feeling secure by focusing on running courses for supervisors and on less than a handful of core products in his chosen sector – the health service. Then the demand for these courses went down and the sector also faced hard times, cutting discretionary budgets wherever it could. So he was left short of work.

His initial plan was to intensify his marketing and to consider dropping his daily rate. On reflection, he realised that he had lodged in a safe and unchallenging rut. He recognised that he tended to be risk-averse and this was what had made him choose the goals that he had. Eventually, he decided that he needed to work in other sectors and to use skills he had learned on a post-graduate course to contribute at an organisational and team level as well as with the development of individuals. He also decided to work with more senior managers. So his goals are about widening his offering as well as widening his network.

Activity

WIDENING OR INTENSIFYING

Do you need to widen your goals or to intensify the skills and activities that you are currently undertaking?

Check your work goals and see if the majority of them are 'more of the same'.

If they are, ask 'Is this a realistic analysis of the situation, and how I should respond?'

Does it represent your tendencies and preferences, and is that why it may not map on to what is needed in your organisation or in the wider market?

On the other hand, if all your goals are about pastures new, does this represent a restless desire to move on or a lack of persistence?

Should you make sure you attain mastery in what you are doing now before you attempt to scale new heights?

Sandy's CPD log – second part

Having read this chapter so far, Sandy added the following entry to the ten items in the CPD log shown at the end of Chapter 3.

> ## SANDY'S CPD LOG (CONTINUED)
>
> World class me. Seem to be not getting world class anywhere. College, home and work mean that I am just getting by with everything. Need to put emphasis on work, then will be more confident at home and college.
>
> Interview myself. Boss's job. Didn't get. No vision for HR. Not tough enough. Not networked enough.
>
> SPICE goals. Physical – need to be more resilient – biggest exercise is the supermarket run, and kids in the park. Join a gym? Arrgh! Intellect – understand organisation culture and change programme. Why is change so difficult?
>
> Planned and emergent. P = 18; E = 12. Planned in a rather passive way. I write it down but don't do much about it. Don't feel like a warrior.
>
> Modes. I'd like to think I am 4 with bits of 6, but in fact I think I am 3–4; so take more responsibility, widen experience.
>
> Widen or intensify. WIDEN.

Our advice to Sandy at this point is 'Don't panic or feel despondent – you are only part-way through the process and there are plenty of resources in the next chapters that will address the issues highlighted.'

Now is the time to focus on how you can boil down the long list of issues to a set of manageable goals that provide focus and a range of areas for you to work on.

Prioritising goals

There is a need for setting priorities among goals – if you have 20 goals, you have none. Our recommendation is to select about six goals plus or minus two (6 ± 2). We suggest this range because if you have fewer than four goals, your circumstances may change and you may have nothing to work on, as your goals become less relevant. Any more than eight goals tends to spread your attention too thinly.

Activity

SELECT YOUR GOALS

From the lists you have accumulated in working through this book or from other planning processes in your own organisation, select the 6 ± 2 goals that you will work on over the next period.

1

2

3

4

5

6

7

8

The customary cycle is a year, and this fits with most companies' appraisal or performance management systems. But if you prefer a quarterly time frame or a three-year one, then work with that. It is likely that different goals will have different time-frames anyway.

Testing commitment to your goals

Are you committed to achieving these development goals? The answer we expect is 'Yes'. But what does 'yes' mean? Listed below, we give a scale of ten different meanings that the answer 'yes' can have in different circumstances.

Meaning of 'yes':

10   I am utterly committed to this.

9   This is my highest priority at work.

8   This is very important to me.

7   I would like to do this.

6   This is nice to do.

5   You seem to want me to do this.

4   I can't risk telling you what I think about this.

3   I'll pretend to go along with this.

2   I will sabotage this.

1   Over my dead body!

Activity

SELECT GOALS YOU CAN COMMIT TO; COMMIT TO THE GOALS YOU SELECT

What is your current commitment to each of your goals? Give it a number.

If it is less than 10, what could you do to make it higher?

In our experience, if it is 6 or less, you are unlikely to carry it through. Consider choosing another goal, or dropping it altogether.

FORMATS FOR YOUR CPD PLAN

The standard format recommended in the CIPD's Raising the Standard and the CPD scanner is outlined below. We have included some key points about each column for you to consider. These are then further developed in the text below this table.

(1) What do I want or need to learn?	(2) What shall I do to achieve this?	(3) What resources or support shall I need?	(4) What will my success criteria be?	(5) Target dates for review and completion
Be specific – clearly describe what you are planning to learn *Check – is this realistic but challenging?*	*Take account of your preferred learning style* *Detail the specific actions you are planning. Plan a mix of activities*	*The costs in time and money* *Whose support do you need to turn this plan into a reality?* *Support is often essential in making informed decisions and to motivate you to keep on target*	*What will you have learned (learning outcomes)?* *This is the measure to show that you have achieved your objectives*	*The date by which you plan to review your progress or achieve this part of your development plan – be realistic* *Small successes achieved quickly will provide motivation towards longer-term goals*

(1)
This column starts us off with a learning goal, and the argument for this is very strong. If we focus just on activities, then we fail to attend to the crucial question of what we want to take from the activity that we can apply to other situations. However, for some it may be more helpful to start the first column with an action, project or work target, and then use the second column, or perhaps the fourth, to specify the learning outcomes. Remember that the CIPD encourages you to be flexible about the format that you use in developing your CPD plan and we encourage you to use one that suits your temperament, learning strategy and mode of development.

(2)
Emergent learners will find this stage particularly difficult. They will ask, 'How do I know what I'll do until I see what opportunities come up?' Our advice to such learners is to map out the likely activities that look as if they will help from where you are now, but don't hesitate to change the activity column in the light of experience when writing up your review. It is a sign of an active learner and the strength of your strategy that you can grab opportunities as they arise and capitalise on the learning that can be drawn from them.

(3)

Is support just about money and resources, or is it also about emotional or practical support? Emphasising the support needed (particularly the money) makes a hostage to fortune. What if the money proves not to be available? Do we abandon our CPD activities for the year? Our view is that many (preferably most) of the activities in a CPD plan could be delivered at no cost or at least within your own budget to pay for it if no one else will. This is another argument against using courses (long or qualification) as a principal means of development – see Chapter 5.

(4)

Learning outcomes are valuable because we need to be able to generalise from particular experiences if we are to increase our ability to act in an unknowable future. However, do outcomes always have to be in terms of learning? Could they instead be about task achievement if the achievement itself will, for instance, increase our self-esteem? See the comment on (1) above.

(5)

Is there ever a case for not putting a date against your goals? The case for dates is a strong one – there is no pressure to perform if there is no deadline. However, some goals may be 'sleepers' just waiting until an opportunity occurs to take action. Is there a case for not putting dates against these, or is it always advisable to set a review date to see how you are going and whether you want to retain this as a goal? We are inclined to the view that dates are always desirable.

Remember that the CIPD specifically recommends that you come up with your own format for the plan. You are not restricted – it does not even have to be a table. Mind-maps, fishbone (see World class me earlier in this chapter) or other formats can work well too. See Chapter 9 for some ideas about alternative approaches to picturing your plan.

One part-time student, John, came up with a table with some different headings, which he used creatively for his plan. Excerpts from it are given below:

From	To (or towards)	Priority	By
Lone wolf	Team leader or consultant	**High** (seems to be a major 'hang up')	Being a good team member. Remember 'good followers make good leaders'. Understanding why and how people differ will help here
Silent participant in meetings	Active participant and part-time 'process observer'	**High** (part of being a supportive team member)	Observe team dynamics – who speaks at meetings, in which order; whether they support or oppose others. Note my own contribution

John, an HR systems designer, was strongly introverted and he recognised that these steps were not trivial. He saw himself as a 'control freak' and his solitary working was a result of this tendency. His high priorities were part of making a transformation because he was moving from specialist technical work into a managerial role. Because of having a clear sense of being on a journey he found the 'from … to' format fitted his purpose.

Sandy's goals – putting together her two plans and prioritising

Having read Chapter 4, Sandy condensed the long list at the end of Chapter 3 and the additional list at the beginning of this chapter into the following eight goals. Sandy used the 'Meaning of Yes' list to show the level of commitment to each goal.

MY GOALS AND MY COMMITMENT TO THEM

1   Develop clear career goal. 10.

2   Seek support from work for my own development beyond the course. 6.

3   Make more impact in meetings. 8.

4   Understand our change process and why it doesn't work. 9.

5   Get hold of a theory of change that I can use. 7.

6   Be seen as business partner; network more; understand business more. 6.

7   Work with boss on vision for HR. 5.

8   Widen my experience, especially in IR and in change process. 7.

On reflection, Sandy thought that eight goals was too many, so 2 and 7 were dropped, and the commitment to 6 was increased from 6 to 8. You may like to make a plan for Sandy to meet the remaining six goals. You can compare this with the plan that Sandy made, which will be found in the next chapter.

PUTTING IT ALL TOGETHER – STARING UP THE STEPS

Finally, as we hinted at the start of this section, goal-setting alone is not enough. The world rewards action. It is not enough to stare up the steps. We must also step up the stairs. This is the subject of the next chapter. In particular, we shall pay attention to the range of methods that you can use to implement your plan. We spend some time on this because we note that even experienced users of CPD sometimes get fixated on one method – eg using only short courses or learning only from work itself.

REFERENCES

BOYDELL, T. and LEARY, M. (1996) *Identifying training needs.* London: Institute of Personnel and Development.

COVEY, S. (1989) *The seven habits of highly effective people: restoring the character ethic.* New York: Simon and Schuster.

HAWKINS, P. (1999) *The art of building windmills.* Liverpool: Graduate into Employment Unit.

MEGGINSON, D. (1994) Planned and emergent learning: a framework and a method. *Managing Learning.* Vol 7, No 6, June. pp29–32.

MEGGINSON, D. (1996) Planned and emergent learning: consequences for development. *Management Learning.* Vol 27, No 4. pp411–428.

MULLIGAN, E. (1999) *Life coaching: change your life in seven days.* London: Piatkus.

PEDLER, M., BURGOYNE, J. and BOYDELL, T. (1997) *The learning company: a strategy for sustainable development.* 2nd ed. Maidenhead: McGraw-Hill.

Undertaking development activities

CHAPTER 5

INTRODUCTION

In this chapter we focus on implementation, identifying the activities that you might undertake and how you can derive maximum learning from them.

We pay particular attention to the range of methods that you can use to implement your plan. Spending time on this is important because even experienced users of CPD sometimes get fixated on familiar methods. To counteract this, we introduce an opportunity to check yourself against a set of characteristics of a skilled learner.

Frequently asked questions about dilemmas involved in working towards a CPD plan are addressed and a range of possible solutions suggested. We shall begin considering what you might want to write down in your CPD record, but we shall address this issue more fully in the next chapter. Chapter 6 also looks at how you review your development and what you might do at the end of a CPD cycle to record and evaluate your learning.

Sandy's plan

Having thought about the goals that were feasible and where there was real commitment, Sandy prepared a plan for the remaining six priorities. It looks like this:

Goal	How	Success criteria	By when
1 Develop clear career goals	Talk with colleague, Pat, who does this well	Career plan in place before appraisal with boss	End of Q1
2 Make more impact at meetings	Attend Better meetings course	Get permission; attend; talk with boss re contribution	End of Q2
	Become school governor	Get appointed and contribute actively	Start of next school year
3 Get full theory of change	Find readings from tutor and borrow notes from students attending MOLK & CM. Talk with our change consultant at work	Be able to describe our change process and say what else we could do	End of Q3

4 Understand our change process and its difficulties	Talk with change team in HR	Fit their understanding of change into theory. Contribute to plans for developing it	End of Q4
5 Be seen as business partner, networker	Understand business more; engage with briefings and talk with managers in other depts. Read about networking	Be invited to other departments' team events	End of Q4
6 Widen experience in IR and change process	Take on challenging tasks now done by boss – eg disciplines and grievances; get on change group as HR rep	Doing disciplinary interviews Member of change group	End of Q2 End of Q4

Would you have made a similar plan? What different emphasis would you place, and why?

BEING A SKILLED LEARNER

Learning, in our experience, is a skilled process. If we are to achieve the CPD plans we have set ourselves, we need to know about the best ways to do this. The characteristics of skilled learners are that they can:

1 anticipate learning opportunities

2 recognise developmental solutions

3 seek out new learning

4 take risks and innovate

5 seek and accept help and feedback

6 use interpersonal skills

7 be constructively self-analytical

8 make connections between different ideas and different people.

Each of these characteristics is explored below with suggestions as to how you can develop the skills involved.

1 Anticipate learning opportunities

Honey (1998) in his video *Live and Learn* reminds us that learning opportunities come in three forms:

- one-dimensional learning opportunities, often focused on individual study which include reading and writing

- two-dimensional learning opportunities, where there is interaction either through talking or communicating with another person or watching a video

- three-dimensional learning opportunities, where something that is learned in one context is applied to a different context.

A practical way to implement your learning is to look at each element of your CPD plan and decide which sorts of learning opportunity are best suited for achieving that goal. This will heighten your awareness of possibilities and help you to be alert to new learning opportunities when they arise.

Activity

LINKING LEARNING OPPORTUNITIES TO YOUR CPD PLAN

Examine each element of your CPD plan and identify if it is most suited to 1D, 2D or 3D learning.

Make a note of potential learning opportunities that may be open to you.

---

2 Recognise developmental solutions

Some people, when undertaking activities in previous chapters, may have decided that their current work is not what they want to continue doing in the long term.

If your options include seeking another job or working for a different organisation, Ibarra (2002) argues that it is not effective just to work out which career you want, and then to go off and do it. This is because our working identity determines our sense of self and thus defines and limits what we are prepared to consider. Thus, if we are to give our minor interests serious consideration, we need to allow space for them to blossom. From her research, Ibarra identifies three techniques:

- Craft experiments – create new identities on the side and try them out to see if they come up to expectation.

- Shift connection – find people who can help us see what we are becoming – this can be a coach or mentor or it could be a new professional community, or community of practice.

- Make sense – tell stories about what we are becoming rather than what we are already.

Activity

SEEK NEW OPPORTUNITIES FOR DEVELOPMENTAL SOLUTIONS

Consider your CPD plan in the light of Ibarra's research and ideas.

Can you identify opportunities where you can craft experiments, shift connection and tell different stories about yourself?

Include these possibilities in your plan.

3   Seek out new learning

Rose (2000) reminds us that we can accelerate our development by learning in different ways, through engaging both sides of our brain.

Typically, at work we use the left side of our brain, which works in a linear way focusing on logic, language and writing. Rose argues that we can be more effective learners if we also engage the right, creative side of our brain, which focuses on holistic, spatial thinking, using image and metaphor. Some of you may have arranged brain-friendly training courses for your staff, but have you also taken those ideas and applied them to your own work and your own development?

Activity

EXPERIMENTING WITH NEW WAYS OF LEARNING

Take a few moments to assess the methods you use in your learning and development – are they predominantly traditional, right-brained approaches or do you experiment with a variety of methods of learning?

If you don't experiment at present but are open to the possibilities, Chapter 9 describes a range of innovative ways of learning linked to CPD. Identify ways that you could experiment with doing things differently.

---

4   Take risks and innovate

Human beings are famously unreliable in calculating risk. Between individuals we also have widely different tendencies to engage in risky behaviour. Some are risk-averse and others are reckless.

In organisations, individuals seem to take low risks interpersonally – especially with senior people. We hear HR people say things like, 'I went to see the HR director to ask if one of my people, who is going to be promoted to report direct to him, could have an external coach. As I talked about how she was under stress, I could see he was switching off. So I emphasised that the request was about stretch targets in her new role. He approved her having an external coach. What I didn't mention at all was that it was his style and behaviour that was causing her stress and making her look outside for help.'

In this scenario the HR manager does not know whether the director will welcome the feedback, or whether it might be better if the two people got together and did a bit of co-mentoring. So often because we want something and have a narrow and short-term view of our interests, we do not take the risk to explore.

Argyris (1991) argues that this is because we adopt what he calls Model 1 behaviour. This is where we:

■ unilaterally defend ourselves and the other party

■ without advocating candidly our own position or

■ inquiring about the other's view.

He contrasts this with Model 2, which is about:

■ generating information which is seen as valid by both parties

■ free and informed choice as to action by both parties

■ internal commitment to the choices, and constant monitoring of the consequences of its implementation.

Why are our assumptions so difficult to surface? Argyris suggests that it is because they are not only undiscussable, but the fact that they are undiscussable is itself undiscussable! This leads to what he describes as the 'self-sealing' nature of our assumptions. For a method to address this quandary, see the left-hand column activity in Chapter 6.

So if you are risk-averse in this way, what can you do to increase your propensity to use more appropriately risky behaviours?

Clearly, prudence is called for here. Find a relatively safe but untested relationship and experiment by asking about willingness to share challenges and experiences. This seems a powerful way of adding to the allies that you have for your own development.

Chapter 7 offers a framework for surfacing and letting go of assumptions that no longer serve us – letting go of excess baggage.

5   Seek and accept help and feedback

Lundin *et al* (2002: 125) tell a story about the CEO of a roofing company, Tile Tech. This CEO would call every customer when they were done with a job and say, 'This is the owner of Tile Tech and I'd like to know how we did. I want to know the good and the bad.'

Resourceful learners seek feedback even when things are going wrong. In fact, they seek feedback especially when the going is getting rough.

When we were running a programme in an overseas country we picked up a hint that all was not well. Rather than ploughing on, we sought out all the concerns of the participants.

Some of what they said was about the programme as a whole, some was about themselves, and some was directed specifically to things that we had done or not done. The response in each case was to validate their experience as true for them. Where we felt that there was a case to answer, we apologised for not meeting their expectations and said what we intended to do differently in the future.

This dialogue led to greatly increased mutual regard and provided a valuable release of some pent-up feelings as well as leading to a clarification of value differences between lecturer and participants.

Activity

SEEK AND ACCEPT HELP AND FEEDBACK

Consider your programme of work at present and identify which aspects are progressing well and those you are less happy with.

Identify any project or element that could benefit from feedback from other parties involved in the work.

Set up a situation where you can receive constructive feedback – ask each person to tell you what is not working well for them and what they think would work better. This gives you extra valuable information.

---

6 Use interpersonal skills

Ideas of emotional intelligence (Goleman, 1996; 1999) have contributed to an understanding of interpersonal skills and to recognising their power to yield the results that you seek in your development. These are customarily divided into inner and outer self, and awareness and action skills. The four components are illustrated in Figure 8.

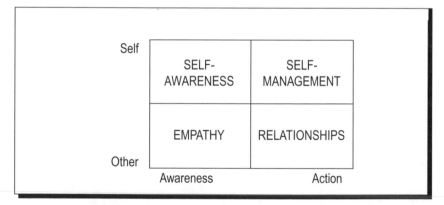

Figure 8 The components of emotional intelligence

Where are your strengths in this matrix, and where are your weaknesses?

Can you access courses, coaching or reading (such as Goleman, 1999) to resolve your weaknesses?

7 Be constructively self-analytical

Many people shy away from self-analysis. An argument that we often hear for this stance is that if you begin this stuff, where will it ever end?

The anti-analysers say that there is so much to do out there in the world that we cannot justify the luxury of time contemplating our navels. Interestingly, most of the highly effective contributors and executives that we know in organisations are also highly reflective.

One effective way to be constructively self-analytical is to assess your time management habits. Procrastination, as we learned in earlier chapters, can be a significant inhibitor of self-development. What will stop you implementing your CPD plan, and what are you going to do to prevent this becoming a self-fulfilling prophecy?

8 Make connections between different ideas and different people

Chapter 8, on networking your future, makes a number of suggestions that may help you with this last in our list of characteristics of skilled learners.

Summary of the characteristics of skilled learners

We have now reviewed eight characteristics of skilled learners. Acting on your CPD plan will depend in large part upon the degree to which you possess and deploy these skills. The activities and questions that we have included with our descriptions of each characteristic are designed to help you to extend your skill as a learner and therefore to maximise what you might gain from undertaking CPD.

METHODS OF DEVELOPMENT

The first thing to say is that there are innumerable methods of carrying out our CPD plan, so the first suggestion that we have to make is to think widely about it. In particular, do not restrict yourself just to short courses.

Here is an example of the first few words in each box in the column 'What did you do?' of a CPD record from an established HR professional:

- Attended a talk …
- Attended a training course …
- Read book …
- Attended a training event …
- Attended a training course …
- Read book …
- Read book …
- Read book …
- Read book …
- Read journal articles …

Now all these activities are laudable and useful in themselves, but we would raise questions about balance. This learning is unduly intellectual and also relatively passive. Where is the learning through doing? Where are the 'working with others' activities? Where is the 'creating one's own experience'?

Another professional clearly had no trouble learning from experience, but in this case she did nothing else. Her comparable list from her own CPD record has just five items over a year:

- Completed a training tender ...

- Project-managed the design of ...

- Oversaw establishment of training administration processes ...

- Developed group training strategy ...

- Undertook training needs analysis ...

Again, all these activities are potentially valuable learning experiences. Are they, however, a full range – or is the author of them simply pulling out the highlights of her last year's work?

Contrast the above with another HR professional in a similar job, whose corresponding list of activities included:

- Co-mentoring with ...

- Managing through change ...

- Planning contribution to ...

- Joined web-group ...

- Consulted self-development group ...

- Attended seminars ...

This list seems to us to be balanced and offers a range of methods, approaches and opportunities for learning.

THE RANGE OF METHODS

There are passive and active methods, solitary and collaborative methods, intellectual and practical methods. Mumford (1997) provides a comprehensive guide to these issues. This is too expensive for most of us to own personally, but is a valuable source if it can be located in a corporate or academic library. The CIPD says in its focus sheets on *The Importance of CPD* that it expects:

> **a balanced mix of activities. These should include professional work-based activities, courses/seminars/ conferences, and self-directed informal learning.**

Here is a range of methods for you to consider under these three headings, with a brief note about the purpose and uses of each.

Professional work-based activities

1 Work project
There are four advantages of discrete projects as learning vehicles. First, they are a focused activity that will come to an end, which signals an opportunity for reflective learning. Of course, this reflection does not always take place, but the opportunity is there for you to take. Second, projects often involve cross-functional working, thus opening up the possibility for developing the skills of a business partner. Third, the finite nature of the project will often give you a clear experience of feedback – either you succeeded or you failed. This feedback from work itself is a valuable source for potential learning. Fourth, projects often involve stretch or new learning for participants. The same can be said for management projects on CIPD courses – and these can be a useful focus for CPD during the study of full-time students.

2 New task
Taking on a wider role or even substituting one task for another is a valuable source of learning. As organisations de-layered through the 1990s, the opportunities for learning through promotion became less frequent. This emphasised the role of taking on new tasks to create new learning. So long as you do not exploit yourself by taking on more than you can bear, new tasks will provide a stimulus for extension of your professional capability, especially if combined with the following item.

3 Mentoring/coaching/co-mentoring
One-to-one helping is a concentrated and effective way of learning (Megginson *et al*, 2006; Megginson and Boydell, 1979). Consider asking someone to mentor you on a voluntary basis, if your organisation does not provide a scheme and you cannot afford a paid helper. Think about what you can offer as a quid pro quo. Alternatively, consider co-mentoring, where each mentors the other on an area of need. (Chapter 8 explores mentoring and suggests guidance on how to set up a mentoring relationship.)

4 Role negotiation (Harrison, 1995)
This framework has proved effective for seeking reciprocal changes. Ask people with whom you work to identify what they would like you to:

- do more of …
- do less of …
- carry on doing (because this contributes to their effectiveness) …

This is helpful feedback in itself. If you then combine it with negotiating what changes you want from them in exchange for what others want of you, then it represents a powerful learning intervention.

5 Benchmarking

Calibrating our own processes and policies against the best that we know sets a horizon for us to aim for. CIPD research reports can provide such data, as can independent research bodies like the Institute for Employment Studies, Industrial Relations Services or Incomes Data Services (www.incomesdata.co.uk).

6 Shadowing

Spend a day with someone who is further on than you in their career, or who has skills that you value, to gain an insight into their work and how they go about it. This can be particularly useful for full-time students who lack HR experience. They may want to link up with part-time colleagues who could thus share their experience in a way that does not place heavy demands on their time. As a quid pro quo the part-time student may value feedback on how his or her effectiveness is seen by his/her full-time colleague.

7 360-degree feedback

Seeking feedback from direct reports, line managers, peers and those you provide a service to is a powerful way of eliciting data. Discussing it with them afterwards is a direct means of acting on the data so generated. You can use a proprietary framework employed by your organisation, or design your own set of issues on which you are seeking their view. Students may want to gather 360-degree feedback from other participants and from staff on their course (see Chapter 3).

8 Giving/receiving feedback

Some organisations provide too much feedback, but in most we do not get nearly enough. Megginson and Pedler (1992, p 65) provide some challenging perspectives on why giving and receiving 'clean' feedback is such a demanding process. The difficulty lies in the feeling that when we have a chance to have our say, we can strike out and show our own superiority. The solution lies in humility and a wholehearted and loving intent to help the other person.

Courses/seminars/conferences

1 Short course

This is the classic method for CPD in schemes that require a number of hours to be totted up each year. It has the advantage of being a specific event set aside for learning. It often suffers from not addressing your specific need directly and from lack of support back at work for implementation. As an active learner, you can take responsibility for ensuring that your learning is applied to work after the course.

2   Qualification

This method is central to the life of many undertaking CPD as part of the CIPD's Professional Development Scheme. However, in our view it should not appear in a major role within a CPD plan or review. We see CPD as being best applied to the rest of your life after the activities and outcomes of the qualification course are registered and taken for granted.

3   CIPD branch activities

Only a fraction of the membership, and indeed only a fraction of the students, in many branches attend these. This seems a pity, as part of our professional development is to become members of a community of practice (Lave and Wenger, 1991). One of the easiest ways of accessing this community beyond our work or course colleagues is through branch, regional and national events.

Self-directed informal learning

1   Biography work

Review the whole of your life using the five questions made famous by Cunningham (1999), or the biography processes of Pedler, Burgoyne and Boydell (1994, pp 11–22). Cunningham's five questions are: Where have I been? Where am I now? Where do I want to get? How will I get there? and How will I know when I have arrived? To these, Fritchie (1990) adds two further questions: What kind of human being do I want to be? and What do I want to do with my life?

2   Change a habit

Some habits are deeply ingrained – whether in personal or professional life. We often require close support when changing or giving up our habits, whether it is smoking or micro-managing staff (see Chapter 7 – Excess baggage, for additional guidance). Rewarding ourselves for progress and setting a target of just 30 days for practising or avoiding the habit are useful incentives to making it happen. Close, frequent contact with a coach or colleague to review progress can also help.

3   Webgroups

These can eliminate barriers of time and space, enabling you to connect up with anyone on the planet who is willing to get together with you to discuss shared interests. Many authors have a webgroup of readers and other authorities when their books are first published, and you may want to approach publishers of authors who you would particularly like to study in some depth. There are also forums for those sharing practical interests.

4   E-learning

The Net is an endless source of information, although much of what you find there is not warranted knowledge so there is just as much spurious nonsense as there is real wisdom and nuggets of valuable information. Using search engines like Google can help. Starting from a respectable website and following links can also be a useful tactic. Online bibliographies, such as Emerald and the CIPD's own service are valuable, and there is a CIPD report on what makes e-learning work available to download at www.cipd.co.uk/changeagendas

5 Action learning/self-development group

Sometimes set up as part of professional courses, these small self-help groups are powerful learning places whether facilitated by a non-member or self-facilitated. If your course does not provide one, or you are not on a course, then consider setting one up for yourself. (Chapter 8 provides further details of action learning and self-development groups.)

6 Reading

The classic passive learning method, but it can be made active by reading with a purpose. Spend time identifying what you want to know or be able to do as a result of the reading, and, with books, use the Contents page and index to find just what you need. Remember to explore www.cipd.co.uk/bookstore. Also pay particular attention to the research reports that the CIPD offers. These include Executive Briefings which (to choose two relevant to the topic of this book) include *Developing Managers for Business Performance* and *The Future of Learning for Work*. The CIPD also publishes Research Reports, which are more in-depth investigations, and there there are many topics of relevance to CPD, including *360-degree Feedback and Culture*, *Competency Frameworks in UK Organisations*, *How People Learn*, *Pressure at Work and the Psychological Contract* and *Training for the Knowledge Economy*. There are discounts on the price of these documents for CIPD members.

7 Teaching someone else

This method is a well-known way for deepening and making explicit your own knowledge of a subject.

8 Networking

See Chapter 8 for suggestions on using this as a learning intervention.

9 Sabbatical

Up to 40 per cent of firms employing professionals use sabbaticals to retain staff who may not have anything to do during a downturn but whose skills may be valuable when work picks up. Individuals can use this time in a huge range of ways. For example, they can achieve a cherished dream, or contribute to education or the provision of services in needy communities at home or overseas.

Activity

CHOOSE A RANGE OF ACTIVITIES

Select a range of activities that you will use to address the goals that you have prioritised in your CPD plan. Allocate the appropriate method or methods to each goal. See if you can include one or two methods that you have not experienced before so that you can widen your experience of learning.

Research by Rothwell and Arnold, 2005, asked CIPD Chartered Members and Fellows about which of 31 methods of development they used in their CPD. They found that the nine most frequently chosen were mostly activities that respondents did in the course of their normal work. Do you view this kind of activity as satisfactory for your own CPD? What might be the motives for HR professionals choosing such methods?

Regular reviews

The difference between undertaking an activity and reflecting upon it is rather arbitrary. Reflecting is very much part of the action. However, in this text we are addressing the activities in this chapter, and the reflection in Chapter 6. Suffice it to say here that in order to make our CPD work, it is useful to have a schedule of regular reviews of your plan. This is the way to keep it alive and to ensure that you maximise the chances of getting development from it.

GETTING THE MOST OUT OF THE EXPERIENCES WE HAVE (FAQS)

In this section we address a number of frequently asked questions about dilemmas involved in working towards a CPD plan, and suggest a range of possible solutions.

Q.1 What if I am content with my job and don't want to devote time to second-guessing what might happen in the future?

In whatever job you are engaged in there will be a need to keep up to date with new legislation – eg employment law update, health and safety. You may also want to improve your understanding of technology or aspects that are not central to your job but are relevant – eg 'finance for non-financial managers'.

You may also be engaged in learning outside of work, and want to develop this. One person's hobby is the restoration of the local branch railway line, and to pursue this he engages in ferocious and constant learning about land ownership, searching out historical records, negotiating with local authorities, and restoring elderly steam engines. Being an active learner in this sort of activity can subsequently have benefits for your work that you may not be able to envisage at present.

Q.2 It's no use my planning. Whatever I decide will have to be put aside when my boss becomes demanding. What's the point in planning when I don't have the chance to realise my dreams?

This person is talking from a very passive position where they are sublimating their own needs in favour of those of their boss's. Refocusing on Chapter 1 – ways in which you might be hindering your CPD – may assist them to change their position and make their own development a priority. Then just do it (JDI) and start with small wins (Pedler and Boydell, 1999, p 44).

Q.3 I've been in the same job for eight years and I really like it. Should I be thinking of changing it, moving on or moving up?

For some people, promotion is important as they enjoy having extra responsibility and a broader span of control. They may also seek extra status and money. Other people may be motivated by different things – enjoying the team they work with, engaging with customers, having the chance to do innovative work.

CPD is not a straitjacket that insists on 'onward and upward'. It is a way of exploring how best you can reach your potential – because we are all unique, we all have to find our individual path.

Q.4 How can I involve my family in my CPD? What I plan can't be done in isolation – their needs have to be considered alongside mine.

Often, when we facilitate courses on professional development we suggest that participants go home and do some of the exercises with their families. One participant contacted us after the course and said that he and his family had a lot of fun planning what they individually and collectively wanted to do in the next three years. They decided that if they achieved their individual and collective targets that they would all go off to Nepal for a holiday – a long-held dream.

Share the ideas in this book with your family and plan your development together.

Q.5 I feel reluctant to engage with the CPD process because my situation is not conventional. We have four young children and I want to spend time with them. My current job is near home, in a beautiful location and allows me the flexibility to pick up the kids. Should I be planning to move and progress?

We spent time with this person exploring all the possible alternatives to his present job. He wanted to move because he recognised that there were few promotion possibilities in his current organisation. By comparing his current job with a range of others he was able to reconnect with those aspects of it that were really important to him. He chose not to move and examined ways of maximising his enjoyment and challenge within his current role. When we saw him recently, some years after our initial discussion, he is still content in his role.

Q.6 My boss picks on me, complains to others about my performance and finds ways of not recommending me for performance-related pay. If I engage in CPD, won't I be giving him another opportunity to get at me?

Our professional development is our own responsibility and our own concern. Some people choose to share their CPD plan with their managers, others do not. CPD is different from appraisal in that it focuses just on you and your future career. Your boss will legitimately talk to you about your appraisal – an assessment of how you are achieving in your present job role.

Q.7 My wife will be very enthusiastic about CPD. She wants me to move from my present job in the public sector to one where I have more status and more money. I have started a Master's degree by distance learning to improve my qualifications, but I am struggling. Would it be a good idea to keep my CPD to myself to avoid extra pressure?

Although CPD is primarily about professional development, it is intimately connected with our personal life and our relationships. Potential engagement in CPD in this instance is touching on some deeper issues related to personal satisfaction.

If we are to be authentic in our professional life, we need to work in a job we enjoy, doing work we feel is significant. Keeping your CPD plan to yourself, in this instance, is a method of avoiding confronting a deeper dissatisfaction between partners, which may be better resolved.

Q.8 I know I am failing at some parts of my job. The only response I get from colleagues is a barrage of criticism which leaves me so demotivated that I haven't the confidence to talk to anyone about how to do things differently.

Start by researching books, videos and tapes on self-esteem. A good starting point would be www.jackcanfield.com.

Then consider who you could talk to, outside of work, to help you to gain a realistic perspective on your situation.

Some suggestions for assisting you to move forward include:

- Visualise yourself achieving a goal for five minutes per day (Pervin, 1989).

- Write a list of what you have achieved each week.

- Share it with a learning buddy on your course on a regular basis.

- Send it to your bosses so they are aware of what you are achieving.

CONCLUSION

This chapter has focused upon undertaking CPD activities. We have looked at what it takes to be a skilled learner; at the range of methods available for development; and at getting the most out of our CPD experiences, which we have addressed through some frequently asked questions.

To conclude, we summarise Sandy's development record of actions against the plan at the start of this chapter. This was completed by Sandy, having read the contents of this chapter and also having had the experiences that came up in the year since the plan was made. Further details about records and what Sandy has written are addressed in Chapter 6.

Sandy's development record

Action against plan	What did I learn?	How I used this learning	Further goals
1 Met Pat – made full plan; looked at my barriers. Attended development centre	Not ready for promotion yet. Set agenda for getting ready. Felt more satisfied at work	Developed my story of my future. Used appraisal to push this with boss	Get boss's support for funds for fast-track development? Must build confidence first
2 Attended Better Meetings course Q2. Became PTA rep – not governor	Not very useful – not enough focus on what I can do. PTA meetings are chaotic and I hate them	Still need to look at my contribution. Getting hold of PTA meetings will help, but need more skill and courage	Would outdoor management development week help? Do I need to change my style?
3 Theory of change. Fellow students gave notes and read them – hard to understand. Tutor recommended 12 books – read Collins (2001)	You have to be there to get it	Able to talk about what we need to do	Still need to have personal experience of doing change – not just reading and talking about it
4 Understand our change – ran session for HR team on Collins	Some people hate theory. We need to start from practice as well as theory	Start selling self on becoming a change team member	Read more; get more involved (need balance of all three)
5 Business partner, networker	Prejudice against HR in some depths is very strong. Can't find any substantial reading on networking. Is it as fluffy as it seems?	Asking for geedback is painful – they tell you. Need to sort what is for me, what is about HR and what is just their problem	How to overcome prejudice against HR. How to make impact when ignored/put down. Push to be invited to team events (combine with 2?)

6 Decided not to pursue IR route – change is the focus for me	Goal became clear once I took action. Boss will support if not too many directions	Keep focusing and clarifying – remember Collins' emphasis on focus; persist	Get on to change team by end of Q2 next year

These notes are brief. What could have been done to make a fuller record? Some of Sandy's frustrations – eg lack of information on networking and models for focusing – will be addressed in Part 3. If you are an experienced professional you may like to compare the (more junior) Sandy's account in these last few chapters with (seasoned professional) Chris's document in Appendix 1. What do you notice about the similarities and differences? We note that seniors tend to learn in and from work, but that they take less time to reflect on their learning. What can you learn from both approaches?

REFERENCES

ARGYRIS, C. (1991) Teaching smart people how to learn. *Harvard Business Review.* Vol 69, No 3, May-June. pp99–109.

COLLINS, J. (2001) *Good to Great.* London: Random House.

CUNNINGHAM, I. (1999) *The wisdom of strategic learning: the self-managed learning solution.* 2nd ed. Aldershot: Gower.

FRITCHIE, R. (1990) Biography work: the missing part of career development. *Industrial and Commercial Training.* Vol 22, No 2. pp27–31.

GOLEMAN, D. (1996) *Emotional intelligence: why it can matter more than IQ.* London: Bloomsbury.

GOLEMAN, D. (1998) *Working with emotional intelligence.* London: Bloomsbury.

HARRISON, R. (1995) *The collected papers of Roger Harrison.* Maidenhead: McGraw-Hill.

HONEY,P. (1998) *Live and let learn [video].* Maidenhead: Peter Honey.

IBARRA, H. (2002) How to stay stuck in the wrong career. *Harvard Business Review.* Vol. 80, No 12, December. pp40–48.

LAVE, J. and WENGER, E. (1991) *Situated learning: legitimate peripheral participation.* Cambridge: Cambridge University Press.

LUNDIN, S., CHRISTENSEN, J. and PAUL, H. (2002) *Fish! Tales.* London: Hodder and Stoughton.

MEGGINSON, D. and BOYDELL, T. (1979) *A manager's guide to coaching.* London: British Association for Commercial and Industrial Education.

MEGGINSON, D., CLUTTERBUCK, D. and GARVEY, B. (2006) *Mentoring in action.* 2nd ed. London: Kogan Page.

MEGGINSON, D. and PEDLER, M. (1992) *Self-development: a facilitator's guide.* Maidenhead: McGraw-Hill.

MEGGINSON, D. and WHITAKER, V. (1996) *Self-development: a facilitator's guide.* Maidenhead: McGraw-Hill.

MUMFORD, A. (1997) *Management development: strategies for action.* 3rd ed. London: Institute of Personnel and Development.

ORAM, M. and WELLINS, R. (1995) *Re-engineering's missing ingredient: the human factor.* London: Institute of Personnel and Development.

PEDLER, M. and BOYDELL, T. (1999) *Managing yourself.* New ed. London: Lemos and Crane.

PEDLER, M., BURGOYNE, J. and BOYDELL, T. (1994) *A manager's guide to self-development.* 3rd ed. London: McGraw-Hill.

PERVIN, L.A. (1989) *Goal concepts in personality and social psychology.* Hillsdale, NJ: Lawrence Erlbaum Associates.

ROSE, C. (2000) *Master it faster: [how to learn faster, make good decisions and think creatively].* London: Industrial Society.

ROTHWELL, A. and ARNOLD, J. (2005) How HR professionals rate continuing professional development. *Human Resource Management Journal.* Vol 15, No 3. pp18–32.

Recording and
evaluating development

CHAPTER 6

INTRODUCTION

This chapter addresses the question of why we need to record our experience of CPD. We start with an overview of reasons for recording. We then explore the value of having both a forward-looking plan and a backward-facing review of progress and achievement. A range of methods of record keeping is explored to assess how they can add value to our CPD process. We conclude with a framework for evaluating CPD.

The basic requirement of the CIPD (and most other professional institutes) is to have a CPD plan and then, one year later, to present a CPD record of what you have done against the plan. This chapter builds on Chapter 5 in helping you to meet this second half of this minimum CIPD obligation. However, making and keeping CPD records is not just about meeting minimum contracts. It is also a key step in any wholehearted CPD effort.

REASONS FOR RECORDING

The process of writing helps us to distil experiences, recognise patterns and discern trends. It enables us to remember what has gone before and capture lessons for the future. It is therefore central to what we learn from the CPD process.

This record is also useful when you are appraised, or for tailoring your CV for a specific promotion or career move. Consultants and freelancers will find it useful when tendering for new work. It can also be kept for CIPD upgrading applications, or in case you are surveyed by the CIPD as part of the Institute's undertaking to the Privy Council to monitor a sample of members' CPD records.

THE CPD RECORD

The starting point for the review that will lead you to writing your CPD record is clearly the goals that you set at the beginning of the period in question. What have you done towards achieving them? What has changed as you went along? Are there any key events that were a crucial source of learning during the period? These events can be formal learning, like attending a course, or having a coaching or mentoring session. They can also be events that happened without planning and which led to some sharp insight, or gave an opportunity to practise and hone a new skill. As a minimum, we need to do the analysis to produce a CPD record once a year.

Doing it more often and keeping and assembling other data will be beneficial for our learning and development. What is 'more often'? Some enthusiasts suggest that five minutes a day (making a note of your biggest learning of the day) is useful. You can keep it online in 'Your development record' on the CIPD's website. Others, like Maureen Scholefield on CIPD's CPD Working Party, suggest once a month, 'at the same time as you fill out your travel expenses'.

Reviewing with support

Corfield (1998, p 66) undertook an evaluation of development planning and review at a large insurance company.

In one small-scale survey, she reviewed the benefits experienced by individuals in having their managers review their development plan.

On a scale of 1 = Partly, 2 = Well and 3 = Extremely well, she found that staff rated these meetings on average as follows:

- The manager gave me ideas – 2.6
- The meeting worked in discussing the benefits of developing – 2.6
- Agreed your goals and what you want to develop – 3
- Agreed what development action to take – 2.6
- Encouraged to use CPD plan – 2.6.

Managers stated that 'staff all appeared to have put a lot of thought into planning for the meeting' (Corfield, 1998, p 67). Managers had few concerns about the process other than having the time to provide coaching and support for individual performers.

The predominant focus of this book is that individuals take responsibility for their own CPD. Corfield's and also Tamkin *et al*'s (1995) work are useful reminders that, in organisations, managers can be engaged in supporting individuals in the CPD process. In college, students can work with tutors and fellow participants.

Working with both plan and record of achievement

It helps to write your record of achievements in the context of an earlier plan. Comparison between the plan and the record is useful for learning. Some CPD evidence that we have seen just focuses on the activities and not on the plans. This is a lack. By setting up a plan, we attempt to shape our environment to meet our aspirations. Of course, the world does not give us everything that we want. Completing the CPD record therefore allows us to make sense of how we relate to this intractable world, and this in itself aids learning.

Activity

REVIEWING SANDY'S RECORD AGAINST THE EARLIER PLAN

Look back at the record of Sandy in Chapter 5 and compare this with the plan in Chapter 4. How did Sandy manage the contrast between plan and outcome? How do you go about dealing with these deviations?

Changing goals

What if you change your goals during the year? We see such change as a fundamental right, and indeed duty, of self-responsible adult learners.

If nothing has happened to us to shift our perspective about where we are going and how we are going to get there in a whole year, then we are either very single-minded or rather inflexible – perhaps both. Alan Fowler (1996, p 56) said:

> **It is not possible to plan all learning opportunities far enough in advance to specify them in a development plan. But CPD should not be so bureaucratic that unexpected events are left unexploited, because they could not be anticipated.**

So, new goals can be added and old goals amended to make sure that they are relevant. Keeping records during the year is best. The learning will be fresher and more cogent.

However, doing it at the year end is still useful – it helps us to chart our progress, to see the direction we are moving in, and it confirms and reinforces newly acquired abilities. It can also indicate to you what kind of learner you have been – active or passive, planned or emergent (see Chapter 4).

Format for CPD records

The format is up to you. Individual approaches are actively encouraged by the CIPD. Records are an opportunity to reflect on accomplishments to date, assess your current situation and coherently plan your future. You may find it useful to have a record of your reflection, reviewing, action and learning.

One list of headings the CIPD offers is:
- Key dates
- What did you do?
- Why?
- What did you learn from this?
- How have you used/will you use this?
- Any further action?

We prefer to put 'What did you do?' in the first column, and number each set of actions in line with the goal in the plan. We then add extra numbers for new goals established during the year.

Of course, you do not have to use this format. The CIPD's website offers you a space for your detailed records of learning from an experience in 'Your development record', which uses the headings 'What did you do?', 'Why?' and 'What did you learn from this?' In choosing what framework to use, the main question to ask yourself is, 'What format gives you the best opportunity to reflect upon and make good sense of the experiences that you have had?'

This leads us into a discussion of reflective practice, which is perhaps the core skill of a developing professional.

LOGGING REFLECTION AND REVIEWING

Journal-keeping creates personal reflective space (Clutterbuck and Megginson, 1999, pp 8–10) and dialogue with self (recognising that my life is worth taking seriously). It allows us to pull out learning and action from planned experience. So keeping some sort of learning journal is key to getting full value from our experience.

Writing your thoughts

A good way to avoid interruption, or at least to limit it to self-interruption, is to write down your thoughts. Keeping a diary or journal seems to have been a strong impulse for people through the centuries. Below we explore some different forms of journal-keeping and illustrate their use in CPD.

1 Personal journal
A dumping ground for everything – retrievable with the 'Find' facility in word-processing packages. In Word this can be used at the level of a file or a set of files within a folder. If you date your entries, this can be helpful when you incorporate some of them into your CPD record. Entries can take the form of learning logs (see below) or be more freeform.

2 Cyclical journal
This helps to know where we are – a reminder for action, a comparator for progress. Cyclical journals are useful for tasks that recur on a monthly or annual basis – like monitoring appraisals. Project logs could follow the project life cycle. They are a key element in many companies' knowledge management efforts (Garvey and Williamson, 2002). It is particularly useful at the end of a project to spend some time reviewing this and writing up your conclusions. Clearly, the review can be usefully done jointly with others (BP Exploration refer to these as 'wash-ups'). Some of the learnings will be individual to you, however.

3 Morning pages
Julia Cameron in The Artist's Way advises starting every day with writing three pages of long-hand notes about whatever you think when you first wake up. Even if it is only 'I can't think what to write', write it! That's why three pages are important. You will rebel if you try writing this for three pages and will find yourself thinking of something else, out of sheer desperation. She says (Cameron, 1995, pp 10–11):

> *There is no wrong way to do morning pages ... . Nobody is allowed to read your morning pages except you. And you shouldn't even read them yourself for the first eight weeks or so ... . All that angry, whiny, petty stuff that you write down in the morning stands between you and your creativity ... . The morning pages are the primary tool of creative recovery.*

We can tell the difference between the days when we write our pages and those when we do not. When we do, we are more focused, clearer, less muddied. There are lots of pressures that make this discipline difficult – early starts, demands of other members of your household. Nevertheless, if you can fit it into your schedule it has been shown to have strongly positive effects.

4 Learning logs
These are useful to do when participating in learning events, and also to be recommended when any striking event takes place that stretches or challenges your abilities. We ask people to note:

- what happened;
- conclusions; and
- proposed action.

When you start writing a learning log, it is fine if you do not know what the learning is from the event, or what you are going to do about it. In fact, this open-endedness can be an advantage. It creates space for you to discover new learning in the act of writing.

Learning logs are the core unit of reflective writing, and any active learner will either write many of them in the course of a year, or have some other mechanism for working on his/her learning from experience. Peter Honey (1994) has gone so far as to say that it should be compulsory to write learning logs. This is one step too far for us. Compulsion vaporises self-development (see Chapter 2).

5 Left-hand column
Argyris (1991) has identified a method of reflecting on experience that powerfully reminds us of our own part in the events and misfortunes that we experience. He calls this method the 'Left-hand column' exercise. A full description of the method is given in Senge *et al* (1994).

The focus of this exercise is an event that we were involved in where we were unhappy about the outcome. We draw a line down the middle of a page, and in the right-hand column focus just on what happened – no interpretation, judgement or commentary. Get it more or less in the sequence that it was said. It will look a bit like the script for a play when you have finished. As you do this it is likely that you will recall thoughts, feelings or impulses to action that occurred to you at the time, but which you decided to suppress.

The next task is to record these choked-off impulses in the left-hand column. Note them where in the conversation they occurred. Was it when you said one thing but were also thinking another? Or when another party was speaking did you notice a feeling welling up inside you, which you did not express?

Reviewing our left-hand columns is a sobering experience. Argyris argues that people do not understand us because so much of what we are thinking or feeling goes unsaid. He suggests that we should learn to use fuller advocacy of our own position and more open inquiry into the thinking of others so that each may become clear to the other.

This is not a trivial undertaking. Keeping left-hand column logs can be a starting point in moving towards this more effective way of being. Individual logs, or a series of them, could lead you to making a plan of how to begin emptying your own left-hand column and how to inquire about the content of others' left-hand columns.

6   Hardback journal/log of all meetings, readings and ruminations
The case for them is that they can be reviewed so as to recall learnings and note dates. They are certainly helpful when doing a retrospective review of a year for a CPD record. One DBA student we know has over 120 of these journals. He is using them retrospectively to analyse his reactions to the scores of management gurus whom he has experienced over the years. He goes back and reads his reflections and reactions that were fresh on the day that he experienced them.

7   Performance log
Many runners keep these, noting mileage and times, and setting up spreadsheets to show cumulative and average performance. Sales people can use records of their calls in a similar manner. If you have quantified targets, it may be appropriate to keep records of progress weekly or monthly.

8   Therapeutic journal/dream journal
Many therapeutic traditions encourage this. You may feel resolved and self-satisfied enough not to need such a practice, just at the moment. It is well to remind ourselves (as the advocate for the disabled said) that 'We are all only temporarily able', so we may need to hold on to this possibility for the future.

9   Dictaphone or tape recorders
As a time-efficient way of capturing thoughts, Dictaphones have a lot going for them. Their problem lies in recovering the data. Two people whom we know who use them extensively for reflection are both superb learners and highly effective performers, but they also have the luxury of a secretary who transcribes their thoughts. Tony Benn, the

veteran UK politician, records daily tapes, which are another example of a creative individual using reflective logging cumulatively to make sense of a lifetime's experiences. As Nancy Kline, 1999, suggests, we can think better if, sometimes, 'we don't just do something, but stand there.'

WHY DOES JOURNAL-WRITING WORK?

Journal-writing works because it is the most direct way we know of forging our identity. And this, it can be argued, is the primary task that we have: to become who we might be.

Part of the power of journal-keeping, in the words of Covey (1990), is that it falls into his Quadrant 2 (see Chapter 4). This includes things that are important but not urgent in our lives. It is only when we are doing things that are important and not urgent that we connect with our purpose and can live in the flow. Journal-keeping helps us to get into this state.

Another feature of words is that they are more concrete than thoughts. When we voice something, it disappears. When we write it – a trace remains. The poet Philip Larkin wrote that the things we do can be ephemeral and disappear or they can live on. What makes them live on, in his view, is our memory, which makes these fleeting experiences harden and give rise to us. Our memories make us what we are. We act on the basis of the accumulated sense that we have made of the world. This does not mean that we are dictated to and simply respond like automata, because, of course, our memories are our experiences to start with, we choose to remember them, and in the course of remembering, we also interpret them and gave them a particular flavour. It is useful to have access to memories and reflections on our past experience, because without them we are condemned to repeat the same errors that we made before. If we can critically evaluate them we stand a chance of changing and growing.

This is the power of retrieved memories, and writing a log is the best way we know to support the retrieving.

Schön (1991, p 243) makes a similar point about the value of reflection in the following extract:

> ❛ Managers do reflect-in-action, but they seldom reflect on their reflection-in-action. Hence this crucially important dimension of their art tends to remain private and inaccessible to others. Moreover, because awareness of one's intuitive thinking usually grows out of practice in articulating it to others, managers often have little access to their own reflection-in-action. ❜

Journal-keeping nurtures an active inner life, and an active inner life seems to contribute towards a considered and considerable external life.

The balance of inner and outer in our lives is crucial for development. Sometimes we need to retreat inwards the better to build ourselves for the next outward step – 'Reculer pour mieux sauter', as Koestler (1970) says. This 'stepping back, the better to leap forward' sustains the inner life, and it also kindles considered self-dialogue about how the balance is going between inner and outer.

We would like to leave the last word on what is necessary in making sense of our world to Weick (1995, p 61), who says that we need:

> **Something that preserves plausibility and coherence, something that is reasonable and memorable, something that embodies past experience and expectations, something that resonates with other people, something that can be constructed retrospectively but also can be used prospectively, something that captures both feeling and thought, something that allows for embellishment to fit current oddities, something that is fun to construct. In short, what is necessary in sensemaking is a good story.**

We explore creating stories as a development method in Chapter 9.

The future of journal-keeping in the e-age

Critics have complained for decades about the death of letter-writing. In many ways, however, e-mail has caused the biggest regeneration in letter-writing since the invention of the penny post.

To give a strong example, two families we know have had children doing development work in the Peruvian Andes. The young people have kept in constant contact with their parents through the Internet café in the nearest Andean village. The series of e-mails from Chimbalumbé represent a wonderful record of a life-changing experience.

Our e-mails, and the folders containing them, are a rich source of data about what we have done and thought. When doing a review we can check through the projects we have undertaken in our warehouse of sent e-mails, to recall to our notice experiences and learning over the previous period.

The option to search electronic journals or data bases is a great advantage – finding a word in a long journal or in a folder of files is very easy within word-processing software. Electronic searching enables us to bring together strands, themes, issues in our lives and reflect upon the movement of our thoughts and feelings. There are qualitative software tools such as Nvivo (www.qsr.com.au) and Visual Concept (www.visual-concept.co.uk/download.htm) that do this integration even better.

There is one dark side to e-journaling. This is the prospect of an all-seeing eye capturing our essence and knowing the deepest recesses of our consciousness. Jacques (1996, pp 117–18) argues that if observation was the control technique of modernism, then 'textualising' (rendering into a file) is the postmodern way. Jacques, however, follows Foucault (1980, p 95) in suggesting that there is no possibility of a Panopticon, with 'them' watching 'us'. Rather, we are a network, an auto-panoptic society:

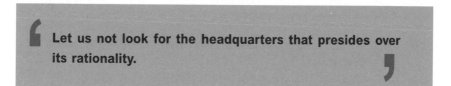

Let us not look for the headquarters that presides over its rationality.

As our journals spin out in their hundreds of thousands of words, we find this thought strangely comforting (Chapter 7 addresses the demonic aspect).

A PORTFOLIO OF ACTION AND LEARNING

Keeping a portfolio of your achievements can be useful for a number of purposes. These could include things that you have produced that give evidence of learning and achievement, and things that others say about you that give their perspective on your performance. Things that you produce can embrace both products of work and outputs of your reflective learning.

Things that you have produced are:

- work projects and reports you have written
- presentations or software you have produced
- video or audio tapes of you in action
- reflective diaries, learning logs.

Things that others say about you comprise:

- certificates, diplomas and qualifications
- testimonials, thanks for contributions and references
- appraisals, 360-degree feedback and performance management data
- evaluations of events you have run.

Note that all these are active records either by you or by somebody else about you. What we do not have here are articles that seemed interesting, programme notes from courses attended and other 'evidence' of passive learning. If you want to record such resources in your portfolio, then write a learning log about them saying what you took from the source or experience, what sense you made of it, and what you did about it. Rothwell and Arnold, 2005, point out that there is a gap between how much we value CPD (mean of 3.76 on a 5-point scale) and how much we engage with it (mean of 2.70 on a similar scale). The gap can be accounted for by the reluctance to reflect and allow the reflections to work on us by recording them. This is the challenge to CPD at a personal, organisational and professional level.

EVALUATION OF CPD

Evaluation is good practice in learning and development of any kind. It is therefore necessary to evaluate CPD. There are a number of features of CPD that dictate the nature of the evaluation. These features are:

- CPD is personal. It can reflect deeply held or deeply felt dreams and aspirations.
- CPD is individual. Each plan starts from the individual's own agenda.
- CPD is ongoing. There is never an endpoint when the job is done.
- CPD is subject to change. The model of having one set of learning objectives at the start and measuring the extent to which they were achieved at the end is not the whole story for CPD.

Because CPD has these features, its evaluation must follow these precepts:

- *Confidentiality respected* – because of its personal nature, some aspects of an individual's CPD may not be for disclosure to others. Even if the evaluator gathers information about these aspects he/she may need to exercise caution about disclosing the source of the information.
- *Individual agenda* – because the data is ipsative (Megginson, 2001) – ie particular to each individual rather than in a general form applying to all – it must be assessed on its own terms. Instead of having a template of outcomes, an approach to evaluation which honours the nature of CPD will ask each respondent to specify his/her own goals for the process and then describe the extent to which the goals were met.
- *On-going* – CPD rolls on from year to year. Estimates are made of what will be done, by when, but these are not hard commitments because such individual projects can be accelerated or slowed down by circumstances. So evaluation is not about measuring the proportion of outcomes that have been delivered, but rather it is about assessing the effects of what has been done.
- *Subject to change* – when people change goals in the course of a year, it is not necessarily a case of failure. Rather, there may be wisdom in changing goals in the light of experience. Evaluation of CPD must recognise that changes in goals are potentially learningful.

The example below offers a strikingly thorough case of evaluation of a major CPD opportunity. To what extent does it match the criteria outlined above? Is there anything that you would do differently?

Wringing the learning out of a major developmental experience

Mark Surtees is an HR professional who dedicates part of his working life to organising expeditions to remote parts of the world, where other busy professionals can take a complete break from their normal activities. They do not sit in the sun, however. Instead, they do some work to support the local community in terms of building facilities for health, education or employment.

Mark has developed a framework for helping each participant to analyse the value of the experience, which is shown below. This has three dimensions that may be of use in evaluating your own experiences.

First, it looks at the range of levels of evaluation from Warr, Bird and Rackham (1970) and Hamblin (1974).

Second, it looks at different aspects of transferable personal learning, building on the framework of Pedler and Boydell (1999).

Third, it offers a set of menus (not included in Figure 9) of possible effects, and it provides a language for describing the outcomes which is grounded in Mark's own evaluation research on earlier expeditions

Level of analysis	Personal development outcomes	Learning to become yourself	Learning to achieve with others	Learning about things – broadly	Learning about things – narrowly	Fun and side effects
Context Person before	Habits and behaviours					
	Beliefs					
	Values					
Inputs	Antecedents					
	Expedition					
Reactions	Reactions					
Output	Learning and job – habits					
	Learning and job – beliefs					
	Learning and job – values					
	Organisation					
	Industry					
	Society					
	Environment					

Figure 9 *Evaluation framework for an expedition*

This framework can be adopted or adapted to explore the conclusions drawn from any major experience. It will help to articulate the learning that is relevant to the rest of life outside the extraordinary situation. It can be applied not just to those once-in-a-lifetime experiences that are set up to shake us and to offer new challenges. It can also be applied to events that just happen that might otherwise be undergone largely as negative experiences such as redundancy or serious illness.

THE CIPD'S STANCE ON RECORDING

The CIPD's stance on recording is clear (CIPD, 2006, p 6). It says, 'There is a set of questions we use when asking you to provide your evidence of your CPD. Answering these questions will help you to explore the pattern of your past and planned learning, with the emphasis firmly on the impact of that learning.' When you submit your results to the CIPD, what you have to focus on is what you did and learned, and what you plan to do in future. The eight questions provide a framework for this description of the outcome of your CPD processes. The questions, with a brief commentary by the authors, are shown in Appendix 2. The CIPD recognises the value as records of your CPD logs, journals or whatever, but they are for your own use. What the CIPD requires is just a summary of these processes by way of responses to the eight questions.

CONCLUSION

In this part of the book we have explored the cycle of CPD from diagnosis to planning to action to reflection.

If you do all this CPD, will it change everything? Of course not, or everyone would do it.

Could it help put more purpose and direction into our life and work? Certainly! Throughout these chapters we have used illustrations from organisations and individuals known to us, and have presented their experiences as we observed or heard them, without elaboration. This represents to us a powerful personal agenda for embracing CPD wholeheartedly.

There is also a coincidence of interests with the CIPD here. The CIPD requires its members to undertake CPD. When we do this with commitment, and a measure of skill, we not only meet the obligations we have to our profession but also differentiate ourselves from those who do not pursue CPD.

Part 3 of this book will assist you to build on this differentiation and consolidate your CPD successes. It offers suggestions for increasing your networks and suggests ways of experimenting with new methods of CPD analysis and planning for your next cycle of CDP.

REFERENCES

ARGYRIS, C. (1991) Teaching smart people how to learn. *Harvard Business Review.* Vol 69, No 3, May-June. pp99–109.

CAMERON, J. (1997) *The artist's way: a course in discovering and recovering your creative self.* London: Pan.

CHARTERED INSTITUTE OF PERSONNEL AND DEVELOPMENT (2006) *Fresh thinking on CPD.* London: CIPD.

CLUTTERBUCK, D. and MEGGINSON D. (1999) *Mentoring executives and directors.* Oxford: Butterworth-Heinemann.

CORFIELD, T. (1998) *An evaluation of the introduction and application of personal development plans at Commercial Union.* [Unpublished MSc dissertation]. Sheffield: Sheffield Business School.

COVEY, S. (1989) *The seven habits of highly effective people: restoring the character ethic.* New York: Simon and Schuster.

FOUCAULT, M. (1978) *The history of sexuality: vol 1: an introduction.* New York: Pantheon Books.

FOWLER, A. (1996) How to manage your own CPD. *People Management.* Vol 2, No 21, 24 October. pp54–56.

GARVEY, B. and WILLIAMSON, B. (2002) *Beyond knowledge management: dialogue, creativity and the corporate curriculum.* Harlow: Financial Times/ Prentice Hall.

HAMBLIN, A. (1974) *Evaluation of control of training.* Maidenhead: McGraw-Hill.

HONEY,P. (1994) Establishing a learning regime. *Organisations and People.* Vol 1, No 1. pp6–9.

JACQUES, R. (1996) *Manufacturing the employee: management knowledge from the 19th to the 21st centuries.* London: Sage.

KLINE, N. (1999) *Time to think: listening to ignite the human mind.* London: Cassell.

KOESTLER, A. (1970) *The act of creation.* London: Pan.

MEGGINSON, D. (2001) *Research as personal unfolding.* Seminar series paper, No 4. Salford: University of Salford. Revans Institute for Action Learning.

PEDLER, M. and BOYDELL, T. (1999) *Managing yourself.* New ed. London: Lemos and Crane.

ROTHWELL, A. and ARNOLD, J. (2005) How HR professionals rate continuing professional development. *Human Resource Management Journal.* Vol 15, No 3. pp18–32.

SCHON, D.A. (1991) *The reflective practitioner: how professionals think in action.* Aldershot: Ashgate.

SENGE, P., ROBERTS, C. and ROSS, R.B. (1994) *The fifth discipline fieldbook: strategies and tools for building a learning organization.* London: Nicholas Brealey.

TAMKIN, P., BARBER, L. and HIRSH, W. (1995) *Personal development plans: case studies of practice.* Brighton: Institute for Employment Studies.

WARR, P., BIRD, M. and RACKHAM, N. (1970) *Evaluation of management training: a practical framework, with cases, for evaluating training needs and results.* London: Gower.

WEICK, K.E. (1995) *Sensemaking in organizations.* Thousand Oaks, CA: Sage.

Consolidating your CPD achievements

In Part 2, you progressed round the CPD cycle, assessing your needs, planning and prioritising your goals, implementing your plans, and reviewing and evaluating your experience.

Part 3 is designed to prevent the possibility of complacency. It stimulates the spiralling of our learning onwards and upwards. We suggest that in addition to reviewing the success of our plan we also need to stand back and look at our progress in a wider context. In a changing world, we cannot do what we have always done or just talk to the people we are familiar with. We must seek variety in both the people we engage with and in the ways that we plan our future CPD.

This part of the book looks at the things that will keep us excited about doing CPD, year on year. If you are working under pressure or are short of time, you may be tempted to pass over this section. We advise you not to because Part 3 enables you to 'sign off' one cycle of development and takes you forward by identifying new people who can assist you in your next cycle of development. It also offers a range of innovative ways of analysing and planning your professional progress.

Chapter 7 helps you to recognise and consolidate your CPD successes. Chapter 8 provides a range of ways in which you can increase your networks. Chapter 9 introduces a variety of new methods for your future CPD analysis and planning.

Celebrating success

INTRODUCTION

Our professional success is a complex pattern of achievements and actions that have been woven together, recorded and evaluated over a period. A weaver we know talks about the importance of knotting the fringe, to prevent the work unravelling over time.

We think that 'knotting the fringe' is an important and often neglected part of CPD. It can help us to create closure before we move on, rationalise our effort, balance our lives, let go of assumptions we no longer need, check our congruence, develop our self-image and encourage others.

FINISHING THE FRINGE

We have identified a number of threads within the fringe that will assist self-developers to consolidate their success. These include:

1   owning our success

2   acknowledging and thanking those who helped

3   addressing the demonic aspect

4   letting go of excess baggage

5   being authentic

6   celebrating completion

7   spreading the word.

In the rest of this chapter, we explore each of these strands in detail.

OWNING OUR SUCCESS

We each define success in different ways. For some people, there are tangible hoops to jump through, like qualifications, promotion or a new job. Others perceive success lying in following a vocation or achieving certain challenges – eg not responding in a negative way when people are being difficult.

It is our response to situations that determines the outcome of the situation, so we can influence both how we define and how we achieve success. We are also in charge of how much of our time is focused on past work, current work in the present, and planning for the future.

Recording and remembering our successes is an important part of our CPD.

Success logs

Do you record your successes so that you can remember them? Some people keep a small notebook on their desk and record each success they achieve. These may not be what other people consider big achievements but they are significant for that person. They may include items like 'Negotiated my next year's workload to my satisfaction' and 'Experimented with my computer and resolved a problem, without asking someone to do it for me'.

It can be helpful at the end of a hard week or at the end of a project to reflect back through your success log and reconnect with those small victories. These entries can also be a way of tracking progress on achieving your CPD plan.

Warm fuzzy files

Jack Canfield (1990) created this term for the place we keep all the feedback we get from others in our professional role. It may be a file or a box: the 'fuzzy' is metaphorical. David comments:

> When I read about 'warm fuzzy files' I thought that this was a splendid idea and I have built them up ever since. They have proved useful when I have sought promotion within the university, when I have applied for upgrading within the Institute, when I have been preparing for my annual appraisal. They have also been invaluable when we have prepared our new brochure for the courses we run. Verbatim quotes have been pulled out of unsolicited e-mails and (with the permission of the authors, of course) been incorporated into the publicity material about our courses.

An argument against starting a warm fuzzy file is that it would be depressing to open one because there would be nothing in it after years of sitting there reproachfully on the shelf. Someone who one of us mentors made this objection, but eventually decided to give it a try. He was surprised and delighted to discover that he soon acquired several e-mails and letters, cards and hand-written feedback sheets. (We suspect that of course he was receiving this feedback before but hadn't given it priority and attention.)

This person found that the contents of his warm fuzzy file were reassuring. He re-read them in the evening when he was faced with a challenging activity on the next day, to remind him that he was capable and was valued by people he worked with.

ACKNOWLEDGING AND THANKING PEOPLE WHO HELPED

Warm fuzzy files are good for collecting feedback from others. It is also important to give feedback as well.

Rosabeth Moss Kanter (1988), the American HR consultant, writes a regular article for a US professional magazine. She decided to include a seasonal theme one December and wrote on the importance of saying thank you – something that costs nothing and is very effective. Her mailbag was overflowing with responses – people commenting on both how important it was and how rarely it happened in their organisations. She was even asked to run a training course on saying thank you, for an organisation where saying thank you was showing too much emotion.

To be skilled communicators, we need also to ensure that our thanks have been heard. Some people find positive feedback difficult to take, so they may screen it out. Repetition may be important in such cases.

Acknowledging and thanking does not have to be verbal. Liz Cross, one of the successful managers in Vivien's book on *Managing People* (Whitaker, 1994, p 114) talked about her commitment to her staff:

> **The ESF [European Social Fund] bid I've been sweating over for the last week has now been typed and printed. The front page names all those who have helped me to put together the information for the bid. I take a copy to each team leader and contributor so they can see what their effort has helped to produce.**

> **Activity**
>
> NEW WAYS OF THANKING PEOPLE FOR CONTRIBUTING TO YOUR CPD
>
> Brainstorm and create a spider diagram or list of all the people who have assisted you with your CPD.
>
> Check that you have both recognised their contribution and thanked them for it. Consider new ways that you can thank people who support you on a regular basis.

Thanking people for their contribution to your CPD is good for them and good for you, as it is a form of closure – a way of moving on.

ADDRESSING THE DEMONIC ASPECT

Some writers talk about the shadow side and others refer to the demonic aspect. Pedler and Aspinwall (1998: 66), when exploring this issue, comment:

> **The demonic emerges from any good idea taken too far.**

They argue that there is a danger that we can overdo our emphasis or focus on something. They go on (1998, p 68) to explain:

> **Any good idea either fades over time or becomes stronger but somehow distorted, the result of too much of a good thing. Thus excellence can degenerate into complacency, and the order and structure of bureaucracy – Max Weber's ideal organisational model – can become rigid and compartmentalised. These 'doubles', or distorted forms of what were originally good, mirror the forces of disorder and decay found in the physical world.**

How does this relate to our CPD? It has something to say about how we approach our new challenges. Typically, when we encounter a new idea we are full of enthusiasm and want to focus on it to the detriment of everything else. Knowledge of the demonic aspect argues for caution and balance.

Jenny, a talented and enthusiastic young professional, purchased a dance mat linked to her PlayStation. She quickly realised that by dancing she could burn up nearly as many calories as she did at the gym. Unfortunately, she danced so much that she pulled a muscle in her leg, This stopped her both dancing and also climbing, which was her passion.

Many of us are tempted to do this with aspects of our CPD plan – they are so exciting that we want to do just that, to the detriment of our other responsibilities.

This demonic aspect is that part of us that is attracted by extremes and sudden dramatic changes. Yet we know that planned step-by-step development leads to more reliable incremental change. This is the case for evolution rather than revolution – when something revolves, it comes back to the same place; when it evolves, it transforms.

So we need to double-check our CPD plan to ensure that it focuses on evolution not revolution, and that it is realistic and won't cause burnout from over-stimulation or over-exertion.

Certain personality types may be more prone to experience this demonic aspect. Buchanan and Huczynski (1997, p 152) summarise Friedman's (1974) theory of Type A and B personalities as:

Type A personality characteristics	Type B personality characteristics
Is competitive	Is able to take time out to enjoy leisure
Has high need for achievement	Is not preoccupied with achievement
Is aggressive	Is easygoing
Works fast	Works to a steady pace
Is impatient	Is seldom impatient
Is extremely alert	Is not easily frustrated
Has tense facial muscles	Moves easily and speaks slowly
Constantly feels time pressure	Seldom lacks enough time

They point out that Type A personalities are three times as likely to suffer from heart disease than Type B personalities. We see the links with the demonic aspect more clearly when Buchanan and Huczynski (1997, p 152) go on to comment:

> The typical Type A thrives on long hours, large amounts of work and tight deadlines. These are, to some extent, socially and organisationally desirable characteristics as

are competitiveness and a high need for achievement. However, a Type A is seldom able to relax enough to stand back from a complex organisational problem to make an effective and comprehensive analysis. They tend to lack the patience and relaxed style required of many management positions. A further problem lies in the fact that their impatience and hostility can increase the stress levels of those who have to work with them. **,**

Complacency

Another aspect of the demonic is its relationship to complacency. Strandgaard's (1981) model of change (see Figure 10) can help us to explore this proposition.

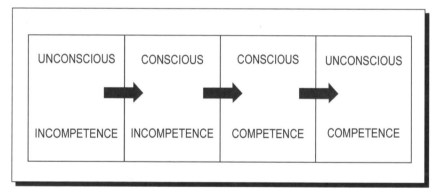

Figure 10   *Strandgaard's model of change*

These stages of development of competence can be related to any skill that we learn – eg driving a car or mastering a new sport. Many of you will have used the model in training sessions to help participants learn about new aspects of their work.

An interesting challenge to this model is to ascertain what happens when you have been in a state of unconscious competence for some time. Is this another situation where the demonic aspect of an idea taken too far kicks in? Is there a danger that when we do things from a position of unconscious competence, we become complacent due to familiarity and lose concentration or focus and slip into bad habits? That somehow we withdraw our energy and stop looking for learning and change in these situations?

CPD can assist us to guard against the dangers of this possible manifestation of the demonic aspect by encouraging us to constantly reappraise everything that we do. In addition, we need to remember the importance of evolution and balance so that we do not suffer from burnout or other consequences of over-exertion.

Holistic success and work–life balance

When we review our successes we need to do so in the context of our whole work–life balance. One way to do this is to assess your life as if it were a metaphorical house with four rooms, a room of the mind, a room of the body, a room of the emotions and a room of the spirit. To achieve balance we need to visit each room within this house, every day.

It is interesting to clarify how much time you currently spend in each room, each day. You can do this by drawing a diagram of your 'house' showing the size of rooms proportionate to the time you spend on these issues. We do this exercise on professional development programmes and have seen a range of odd-looking houses (see Figure 11).

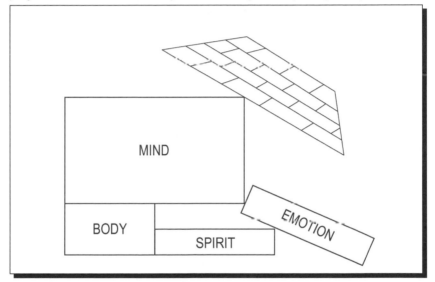

Figure 11   *Current state of metaphorical house*

The next step is then to draw your 'house with four rooms' in the proportions that suggest how you would ideally like to spend your time (see Figure 12).

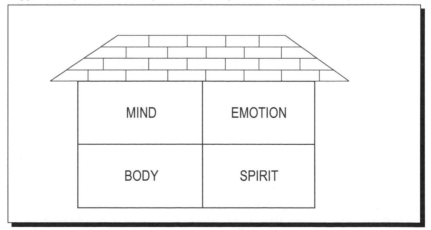

Figure 12   *Desired state of metaphorical house*

Activity

ACTION PLANNING FOR A BALANCED LIFE

Consider the whole of your life using the metaphor of a house with four rooms.

Assess how much time you spend in each room at present and draw your metaphorical house as it appears at present.

Then dream a little. Project yourself into the future and think about how you would like your metaphorical house to be – how big are each of the rooms and how do they compare in size and placing with the other rooms?

When you can look at the differences between your two diagrams, you can then explore how progression towards your ideal can be stimulated.

Do we spend too much time in some rooms and not enough in others? One way to assist our life balance is to consider if there are habits and attitudes we need to let go of – our excess baggage.

LETTING GO OF EXCESS BAGGAGE

As we go through life we tend to take in ideas and take on new tasks or responsibilities. We do not consider whether we need to let go of any of the assumptions, values, responsibilities or ways of being that have become a part of our life.

Sometimes life events such as serious illness or the death of someone close to us interrupt our daily pattern and stimulate us to reflect and re-evaluate. One woman had to re-evaluate her life when she was made redundant. Little support was available to her as she experienced this transition and she felt rejected and vulnerable. Her assumption was that 'she was not good enough' and her reaction to this crisis was to seek a secure job in a large organisation. She strove to work for responsibility and promotion, even though she dreamed about doing leading-edge research and maintaining work–life balance. Eventually, after a series of stress-related illnesses, she recognised that she could let go of her feelings of rejection – that actually she was a talented, multi-skilled professional who could have a portfolio career if she wished. When she acknowledged this and let go of her bad experiences of redundancy and her old habits of seeking security, she was able to reject extra commitments which once would have seemed an honour, and enjoy her life much more.

A very talented HR consultant was exploring his CPD and recognised that he had what felt like a major block to his self-development. He explained that it felt like literally 'being branded' a failure – a metaphorical tattoo on his arm. The event that changed the course of his life was failing to pass his exams to get into a good school. He made assumptions that he was not intelligent or academic. Consequently, he tried to avoid anything to do with exams or writing things down. As he engaged in CPD and asked for and gained feedback from both the participants on his courses and his colleagues, he recognised that his long-held assumptions that he was a failure and not intelligent were inaccurate. He was then able both to develop confidence in report-writing and register on a Master's degree as a mature student and enjoy his studies.

So it can be helpful to stand back and reflect on both your professional and personal life. Checking out assumptions and old habits can help you to clarify that you are really getting what you want and need in terms of your development.

Most of us are unconsciously carrying around excess baggage – old 'messages' or assumptions that can stop us doing things, sap our energy or diminish our hope for the future. When we analyse our bad experiences it is often possible to track them back to old habits that have grown out of unresolved issues, which we term excess baggage.

Excess baggage ⇔ Old habits ⇔ Bad experiences

The following series of exercises will help you to analyse your experiences and assumptions and assist you to let go of any excess baggage you may unconsciously be carrying about with you.

Activity

MY EXCESS BAGGAGE CHECK-IN

Complete the following sentences for yourself. Some people may identify pivotal events in their life; others may focus on attitudes or underlying assumptions that have not been challenged which may be hindering self-development. If you have more than one significant event or assumption, repeat this exercise for each experience identified.

The assumption or event that changed the course of my life was …

As a result of this I …

My attitude towards taking risks is …

The unconscious assumptions I made after this event included …

If this event had not occurred I would like to have …

When I daydream I imagine that I could …

If I recognised that I could move on and let go I could …

Consider what you need practically to do to let go and move on. Holding on to something, either physically or mentally, requires a lot more energy and effort than letting go. Yet it is hard to let go of the familiar. Can you change one thing at once? Is it possible to practise being different? One successful entrepreneur we worked with chose to change his style of management. He got up half an hour earlier every day so that he could practise his new management style in front of the mirror before he went to work. Think about who can support you and help you as you let go and make changes.

BEING AUTHENTIC

When we work with students we often ask them to identify the characteristics of their 'best boss' – the person that they most enjoyed working for. One of the popular responses is that the best bosses do what they say they are going to – they are both congruent and consistent – they treat people as they would like to be treated. (Congruence was one of the concepts we discussed in Chapter 3.)

Inevitably, in this exercise we also hear about worst bosses as they seem easier to identify. The students' feedback about these ineffective managers was that they said one thing (or believed one thing) and did another – there was a gap between the values they espoused and what they did in practice (Argyris, 1991).

Activity

ASSESSING YOUR AUTHENTICITY

This is a challenging activity. We can focus on either our professional life or our whole life.

Examine in a thorough-going way whether you work and live according to the values you espouse. Is there a gap between your espoused values and your values in use?

If so, what steps do you need to take to change this?

If we are to be effective in both our current professional role and our future aspirations it is important that there is no gap or distortion between the values we hold and our professional practice.

CELEBRATING COMPLETION

The predominance of the Protestant work ethic in Western societies encourages us to take a serious approach to our working life. Traditional societies, by contrast, understood the importance of ritual in respect of both individual development and group process.

Graduation presentations and parties are ritual celebrations that you have become a different kind of person – the kind of person who can gain a CIPD qualification – and who can go forward and seek promotion and make a difference. Rituals assist us to make these transitions.

How do you celebrate the achievement of your CPD plan each year? Do you share your successes with your colleagues? Do you invite people to a celebratory lunch? Many people choose to keep what they are doing to themselves – perhaps seeing it as boastful to make an issue about their achievements, not thinking that colleagues may be interested. A new newsletter was circulated in one organisation and colleagues commented that it was great to hear what everyone else was doing.

Activity

CELEBRATING YOUR ACHIEVEMENTS

Consider your professional achievements over the past year.

Have you taken time to assess them? Who have you selected to celebrate your progress with? Is there more you could do to recognise your progress and your development?

Celebrations do not have to be expensive. They may involve sharing a coffee with a friend or bringing some cake into the office. Their function is to help you to recognise that you have developed and to assist you in moving onward and upward to further development.

SPREADING TIIE WORD

Many of us are shy about discussing our achievements and sharing our aspirations. Our upbringing leads us to believe that boasting is bad and putting ourselves forward is pushy. Marianne Williamson, in words sung at Nelson Mandela's inauguration, says:

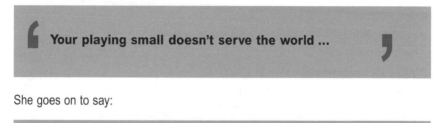

Your playing small doesn't serve the world ...

She goes on to say:

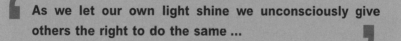

As we let our own light shine we unconsciously give others the right to do the same ...

Talking about your CPD with others can be fun: it may stimulate ideas for doing things differently at work or it may enable you to discover someone else who shares similar interests to your own.

Could you talk about what you are doing in the informal spaces within a CIPD branch meeting? Or suggest starting a self-development group to encourage CPD in your area? In the next chapter we shall look at how to do this.

Activity

SPREADING THE WORD

Think about how you could use your enthusiasm and commitment to CPD to dialogue with others. List possible people you would like to talk to. Identify situations where discussions could take place.

CONCLUSION

In this chapter we have explored ways that you can deepen your understanding and appreciation of your own success so that you can use the energy generated by your success to move on in your journey of self-development.

The next chapter will assist you to examine a range of ways in which you can connect with and learn from others who share an interest in and commitment to CPD.

REFERENCES

ARGYRIS, C. (1991) Teaching smart people how to learn. *Harvard Business Review.* Vol 69, No 3, May-June. pp99–109.

BUCHANAN, D. and HUCZYNSKI, A. (1997) *Organizational behaviour: an introductory text.* 3rd ed. London: Prentice Hall.

CANFIELD, J. (1991) *Self-esteem and peak performance [audio cassette].* Milton Keynes: Careertrack tapes.

FRIEDMAN, M. and ROSENMAN, R.H. (1974). *Type A behaviour and your heart.* New York: Knopf.

MOSS KANTER, R. (1988) 'Dr Kanter plays Atlanta.' *Business Matters.* London: BBC.

PEDLER, M. and ASPINWALL, K. (1998) *A concise guide to the learning organization.* London: Lemos and Crane.

STRANDGAARD, F. (1981) *NLP made visual.* Copenhagen: Connector.

WHITAKER, V. (1994) *Managing people.* London: HarperCollins.

WILLIAMSON, M. (1996) *A Return to Love: Reflections on the Principles of a Course in Miracles.* London: Thorson.

Networking your future

INTRODUCTION

> A very successful management coach had many clients within a large organisation. A crisis in the financial world caused the organisation to collapse and the coach lost 90 per cent of his business and plans for the future.
>
> A principal training officer in the public sector was developing many exciting ideas with the chief executive and had built a strong relationship with him. These plans were in jeopardy when the chief executive was suddenly removed.

Networking is not just about recognising the connections we have with others; it is also about making the most of these connections. It is something we can all do, at any time. We have the opportunity to connect with each other whenever we talk – through face-to-face conversations, meetings or phone calls – and whenever we write – through e-mail, letters, proposals or reports. Networking can add value and expand our horizons (Whitaker, 1995).

This chapter will help you to identify who are the key people you need to communicate with about your CPD, both now and in the future. It will reinforce the value and importance of expansive networks. Some of us have a few key people or clients whom we depend on. If we operate like this we make ourselves vulnerable.

We shall begin by encouraging you to analyse your current networks. We shall then provide practical suggestions about how to enhance your existing networks and create new ones.

ANALYSING YOUR CPD NETWORK

Think for a few moments about the people you currently talk with on a regular basis about your own professional development – partner, friends or family, colleagues at work. Then think of people whom you might like to converse with in the future. The following different types of network may assist you to add to your initial ideas:

- Formal network – your manager, members of your team, links with your professional association or trade union, formal mentoring relationships, course tutors.

- Informal network – people you lunch with, develop ideas with, people you seek help and advice from on an informal basis.

- Academic network – tutors and fellow students on your course.

- CIPD network – colleagues you meet regularly at local, regional and national CIPD events. Branch interest groups, often consultants' networks, are also useful forums, where people have strong shared interests. Rothwell and Arnold, 1995, emphasise the importance of professional identification as a precursor to valuing CPD.

- Potential or future network – people you want to be like, people who hold the type of job you aspire to, people within your professional association who could assist you in developing your skills, knowledge and plans.

- Dream network – people who have done what you dream about doing. They may be successful professionals in your specialism and in your area of work (overlapping with the networks listed above). Alternatively they may be national figures in the profession or speakers at conferences that you have attended. They may be big names in another country or continent.

With some of these networks (especially the last) it can be daunting to approach members. Could you seek their support? What could you offer them? Our personal experience has included both seeking out such contacts and also (as published authors) being sought out by them. Thinking about the experience from both points of view, we would offer the following advice for creating a dream network.

First, do not be afraid to ask. If you are rejected, don't worry. You are no worse off than you were before you tried. Then you did not have someone in your network. You still do not have anyone. You are no worse off. You may expect to feel worse off, devastated by the rejection, but this is just your own internal negative self-talk. Think of all the other people who might be useful to you and have a go at contacting some of them.

Second, be explicit about what you seek, and make it relatively modest. Public figures often have concerns about taking on open-ended commitments, so be explicit about what you want and then be prepared to modify this if the contact says, 'I am not prepared to give you that, but I will give you this.'

Third, ask if there is anything that you can do in return. Writers, in particular, often want their ideas testing out with groups of potential users, so if you have access to such people – through a course you are attending or from work – offer this, and say that you will write up the results and send it to them.

Finally, do your homework. If the target of your attention has written or made public speeches, get hold of the text and approach them as an informed and interested inquirer rather than simply a professional networker.

Activity

DRAWING YOUR CPD NETWORK

Take a large sheet of flipchart paper and six different-coloured pens.

Draw each of your networks, as outlined above, using a different-coloured pen for each network. Write in the names of all the people in each network.

Identify the people who appear in more than one network.

Now you have drawn or listed your current networks, consider how you could develop your networks further.

Questions to help you to develop your CPD network

Are there key people you rely on a lot?
Could you diversify your contacts? Why not aim to double the number of contacts that you have?

Can you identify people with whom you would like to make contact but haven't yet found the time or courage to?
Add them to your future network. Who could help you to make contact with them? Do you have a mentor or more experienced manager who could help you to develop your external networks? If not, how could you find one?

Are your networking relationships of value to both parties?
If not, is there a way of making them mutually beneficial?

Do you use lack of time as an excuse for lack of reflection and not talking to your contacts?
How can you set aside time among the immediate day-to-day pressures to focus on your potential in the future?

When planning your next career move are you able to identify people who are currently in a job you would like, and go to talk to them to find out more about the post?
Add them to your future network. Identify contacts who might introduce you to these people, if this is necessary.

How do you use your external networks to learn about other people's good practice and new ideas? How do you publicise your own good practice and develop new ways of working?
Can you set up a learning network with colleagues, where you share learning and good practice on a regular basis?

Activity

CREATING YOUR FUTURE CPD NETWORK

Take a seventh different-coloured pen.

As you work through the list of questions above, add to your existing CPD network by adding to current networks, or by creating a new one.

Then create a pragmatic action plan to outline what you need to do to make your future network a reality. Specify:

- What?
- Who?
- By when?

CREATING A LEARNING NETWORK THROUGH ACTION LEARNING

Action Learning was developed by Reg Revans (1998). It is based on the premise that:

> **There can be no learning without action and no (sober and deliberate) action without learning.**

Revans (1998) recognises that everything and everyone is constantly changing and suggests that individuals cannot develop unless their rate of change is equal to or greater than the rate of change being experienced around them.

He also argues that this learning is more likely to occur if people are working on an issue or task that they want to do something about – take action on. This conscious process of learning can be deeper and potentially more transformative than our everyday unconscious patterns of learning.

$$L = P + Q$$

Revans (1998) identifies two elements of learning (L) – traditional instruction or programmed knowledge (P), and critical reflection or questioning insight (Q).

Programmed knowledge

Revans (1998) makes a distinction between puzzles and problems. Puzzles, like jigsaws, have a right answer – only one way of resolution. They can be solved by the application of programmed knowledge with the help of experts. Problems, in contrast, have a range of possible solutions that can be developed through questioning insight.

Critical reflection or questioning insight

Ever since Donald Schön wrote *The Reflective Practitioner* in 1983, reflective practice has been on the agenda for people who are serious about developing themselves.

Schön proposes (Schön, 1991, p 130) that 'by attending to the practitioner's reflection-in-action … it is possible to discover a fundamental structure of professional inquiry', which underlies the many varieties of professional practice. As we understand it, Schön's prescription for professional practice, grounded in his close attention to how professionals reflect in action, adopts the following lines:

- Each case is treated as unique, it cannot be solved by applying standard theories or techniques.

- Problematic situations must be reframed.

- Before deciding how to solve the problem, professionals consider whether it is a problem worth solving and what role the practitioner should play in its solution.

- Professionals respond to complexity with spontaneity and artistry – which includes deciding which aspects of the mass of information available they attend to, and holding several ways of looking at things at once without disrupting the flow of inquiry.

In short, professionals conduct a reflective discussion about a unique and uncertain situation.

Bolton, focusing on staff in health and social care, suggests (Bolton, 2001, p 14) that reflective practice can enable us to:

- study our own decision-making processes

- be constructively critical of our relationships with colleagues

- analyse hesitations and skill and knowledge gaps

- face problematic and painful episodes

- identify learning needs.

So she sees the reflection as being more diagnostic, more to do with planning, than Schön does.

Clutterbuck and Megginson (1999, pp 8–10) describe the phases in the reflection process as:

- disaggregation

- framing

- implication analysis

- insight

- reframing

- options

- action.

This model emphasises the change in energy level that accompanies working through these processes. Outer energy falls as we go more inward to the point of insight, and then rises as we move forward into action.

Reflectivity can be an individual, paired or group activity. Revans (1998) argues that maximum benefit can be gained from working as a group or set, because this can offer a wider range of suggestions or options than working alone or with a mentor.

In our experience, this option works well when there is a high level of commitment, trust and co-operation within the set. A skilled and experienced set adviser can facilitate the development of these dynamics.

Action Learning sets

Members of such groups or sets, which focus on reflectivity and conscious learning:

- commit to a number of meetings
- explore problems that personally engage set members in their day-to-day work or their professional future
- review assumptions of current practice
- develop alternatives for action through supportive and challenging questioning
- reflect on action taken in the light of new insight
- share individual perceptions of the impact of further action
- learn about three aspects: about the problem being resolved, about themselves as learners, and about the process of learning itself.

Sets as part of a CIPD qualification

In some CIPD-approved academic centres the work on CPD as part of the qualification is done through action learning sets. We have experience of working with full-time, part-time and also mixed student groups in this way.

These sets can be valuable in that they give each member half a dozen or so other perspectives on how to go about learning. As people talk about their own CPD, the other members begin to appreciate that there are some aspects that the speaker focuses on and others that he/she neglects. Supportive and challenging feedback from the rest of the group can assist them to widen their approach.

For example, in one set we had six individuals who initially concentrated their CPD planning in the following ways:

- The first focused everything on modules of the course.
- The second addressed only skill issues concerning their current job.
- The third gave all their attention to a big challenge, which was that they were on temporary promotion and that they had just three months to make an impact before it could come to an end.

- The fourth looked at future career and paid attention to the next job that they wanted.

- The fifth took a very long-term view of where they wanted to get to eventually.

- The sixth adopted a balanced view, looking at work, home and community.

Each of these approaches to CPD planning is legitimate, but it is so much more empowering to have role models for all six approaches being worked out in front of you.

Another direction in which learning sets can take professional development is towards inter-organisational learning (Mann et al, 2004). Learning sets, if they continue for some time, can also evolve into self-developments groups, as described in the next section.

CREATING YOUR OWN SELF-DEVELOPMENT GROUP

On a number of occasions we have had the privilege of working with groups that have been committed to their own development and have continued to meet on a self-development basis after their formal facilitated sessions were over.

Three of these took different forms, so if you are interested in this option you may like to consider the range that they illustrate. Or, indeed, you may have quite other ideas for your own group.

The first group's members were full-time students, and formed around their MSc dissertations. When they came to the end of the taught part of the course, they initially felt that there was no point in continuing to meet because their dissertations were essentially individual projects. However, after further consideration, and after sharing the feelings and concerns that they had about the process, they decided that they had a range of needs. They needed support, ideas, references, an opportunity to share and review drafts of chapters, and especially a chance to share the challenges of practice in contributing to the change process that was the focus of their research. This group continued right through to seeking and starting new jobs, and finished only when members moved to different parts of the country.

All the members of the second group were part-timers, specialising in one aspect of the course. They had studied a number of optional units together. Their shared professional interests and their passion for learning meant that they were prepared to continue meeting during the dissertation phase and thereafter, principally to share ideas and enthusiasms about professional practice.

The third group was a mixture of full-time and part-time students. After the full-timers finished the taught part of the course, the part-timers recruited second-year part-timers from other sets to join them. They agreed to continue reflecting and supporting each other in reviewing their progress on their CPD plan. They also addressed work problems that they had started to share during the formal part of the group's existence.

If you would like to read about setting up and managing these groups, Megginson and Whitaker (1996, pp 69, 75–80) and Megginson and Pedler (1992, pp 4–8, 38–41) have suggestions about how to proceed.

Activity

SETTING UP YOUR OWN SELF-DEVELOPMENT GROUP

Consider if you would like to set up your own self-development group to continue learning in the rest of your course, and perhaps afterwards.

What would be the focus of your group? How would you select members for it? Who would take responsibility for this? Would you need facilitation help, or, if not, how would facilitation roles be shared in the group?

LEARNING PARTNERS – MENTORING

One-to-one dialogue may also have an important place in your development network. Many organisations operate mentoring schemes. Alternatively, informal arrangements can be either internal or external to the organisation.

Mentoring is defined as:

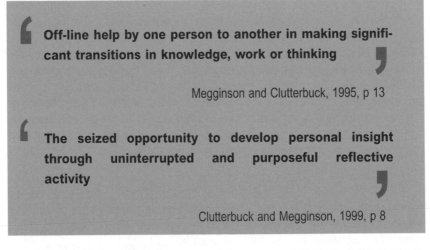

Off-line help by one person to another in making significant transitions in knowledge, work or thinking

Megginson and Clutterbuck, 1995, p 13

The seized opportunity to develop personal insight through uninterrupted and purposeful reflective activity

Clutterbuck and Megginson, 1999, p 8

From their research in *Mentoring in Action*, Megginson and Clutterbuck (1995) identify four key roles in a mentoring relationship:

- improve performance
- career development
- counsellor

■   share knowledge.

This research also suggests that the most successful relationships are mentee- or learner-driven. Mentoring is seen as a means to connect with one's own voice, starting with articulating the learner's dream.

The dynamics of a mentoring relationship develop in a balanced way when there is 'clear water' – that is, there are no additional elements in the relationship – eg line management responsibility. Historically, a mentor was perceived as an older, more experienced person. The possible disadvantage of such a relationship is that, in Transactional Analysis terms, the relationship may tend towards that of Parent–Child rather than an assertive Adult–Adult relationship, driven by the learner.

Mentoring relationships typically develop through a number of stages:

■   identifying and approaching a range of possible mentors

■   establishing a 'match' between mentor and learner

■   clarifying expectations of learner and mentor

■   agreeing the purpose and duration of the mentoring relationship

■   planning a location for relaxed, confidential, uninterrupted dialogue

■   developing vision, monitoring progress and celebrating achievement

■   evaluation of relationship and future plans for contact.

Activity

ESTABLISHING A MENTORING RELATIONSHIP

Consider whether it would be helpful for your CPD to seek a mentor who could assist you with your professional development.

Do you want a mentor within your organisation? If so, contact whoever organises formal or informal mentoring schemes.

Many people prefer to have a mentor who is external to their organisation, as they want to think beyond their present job and possibly beyond their current organisation. Brainstorm a range of people you may like to approach, not forgetting those people in your dream network and future network.

Then follow the above stages, also including suggestions made earlier in the chapter.

FIVE DEGREES OF SEPARATION

In this chapter we have explored how to widen and deepen our networks so that we can achieve the things we dream about. Some people may feel daunted by the possibility of networking. Networking is not just for the confident and the extrovert: everyone can do it with a little courage and practice.

What is heartening, from our own and others' experience, is the widely observed phenomenon of 'five degrees of separation'. This suggests that it is possible to link every professional anywhere in the world with any other professional by a chain of acquaintance no more than five links long. What is more, professionals are good at finding these links by skilful questioning. So we can network with anyone we want to, and it will typically take less than five contacts to make the connection.

As an example, we were recently introduced to a senior manager from the national telecom company in Venezuela. We soon established that she knew an ex-student and good friend of ours, who works in HR in Venezuela. We were delighted to be able to hear of his progress, and to obtain his current contact details. This was a case of one degree of separation.

So it is always possible to extend and to re-establish networks.

HOW TO ORGANISE AND ENCOURAGE CPD

Recent work in coaching (Clutterbuck and Megginson, 2005) shows that with one-to-one development it is necessary to hold an organisational perspective if you want to introduce system-wide change. Transforming these findings to the field of CPD suggests that HR leaders should link CPD to business drivers; encourage seniors to do CPD; provide CPD training; reward and recognise CPD; adopt a systemic perspective; and ensure that the move to CPD is managed (Clutterbuck and Megginson, 2005, p 28). The increasing rate of obsolescence of professional knowledge (Van Jaarsveld and Batt, 2002) makes this a priority for professional-service organisations and for professional functions in all organisations. The emphasis needs to be placed on learning from experience and not simply on counting the hours (Blyth, 2000).

In an insurance company where we designed and implemented an extensive CPD programme we found that it was useful to train line managers to support the initiative, but also to have CPD champions on each site who were trained and supported so that they in turn could support the busy line managers in this task. These champions were found to best come from the line, rather than from HR. In this initiative we also found that it was helpful to have high-quality unambiguous materials available to all, offering a framework for reflection and planning of CPD.

CONCLUSION

Analysing your networks and extending them gives us more resources to progress our CPD. Action learning and self-development groups, mentoring relationships, and just opening up the opportunities we come across, are all tools for extending this range of learning alliances (Clutterbuck, 1998).

In the next chapter we recognise that CPD planning is something that we shall be doing on an annual basis. We explore a range of different ways of undertaking this process, so that we can incorporate variety into our CPD planning.

REFERENCES

BLYTH, A. (2000) Count the value not the hours. *The Architects' Journal.* Vol 53, 17 February.

BOLTON, G. (2001) *Reflective practice: writing and professional development.* London: Paul Chapman.

CLUTTERBUCK, D. and MEGGINSON D. (1999) *Mentoring executives and directors.* Oxford: Butterworth-Heinemann.

CLUTTERBUCK, D. and MEGGINSON, D. (2005) *Making coaching work: creating a coaching culture.* London: Chartered Institute of Personnel and Development.

CLUTTERBUCK, D. (1998) *Learning alliances: tapping into talent.* London: Institute of Personnel and Development.

MANN, P., PRITCHARD, S. and RUMMERY, K. (2004) Supporting organisational partnerships in the public sector. *Public Management Review.* Vol 6, No 3. pp417–439.

MEGGINSON, D. and CLUTTERBUCK, D. (1995) *Mentoring in action.* London: Kogan Page.

MEGGINSON, D. and PEDLER, M. (1992) *Self-development: a facilitator's guide.* Maidenhead: McGraw-Hill.

REVANS, R.R. (1998) *ABC of action learning.* London: Lemos and Crane.

ROTHWELL, A. and ARNOLD, J. (2005) How HR professionals rate continuing professional development. *Human Resource Management Journal.* Vol 15, No 3. pp18–32.

SCHON, D.A. (1991) *The reflective practitioner: how professionals think in action.* Aldershot: Ashgate.

VAN JAARSVELD, D. and BATT, R. (2002) Changes in employment and working conditions among technical and professional workers. *Proceedings of the 54th Annual Meeting of the Industrial Relations Research Association.* Madison, WI: Industrial Relations Research Association.

WHITAKER, V. (1995) Networking. In: CRAINER, S. (ed). *The Financial Times handbook of management.* London: Pitman.

Empowering career creativity | CHAPTER 9

INTRODUCTION

CPD is a continuous and continuing process. For many of us, creating our CPD plan will be an annual event. So, in this chapter, we shall explore a range of creative ways of engaging in CPD.

Choosing a different method of analysing and creating your CPD plan each year is excellent in time management terms – a 'double whammy'. By using a new method, you are enhancing your knowledge and skills at the same time as you are considering other areas of knowledge and skills that you need to develop.

We shall use NLP to assist you to identify whether you are an auditory, visual or kinaesthetic learner, and provide appropriate creative ways to diagnose and plan your future development needs for each of these orientations.

In addition, we shall explore ways to refine your skills in analysis and planning so that you keep motivated, intensify your focus, and are continually open and eager for change.

USING OUR SENSES TO ENHANCE OUR LEARNING

NLP has assisted us to become more aware about how we use our senses in learning. Research has identified three ways that we take in and process information and communicate with others. These are:

- auditory
- visual
- kinaesthetic.

Genetic inheritance and environmental experience may result in individuals developing a preference for one of these orientations.

We can clarify our sensory preferences by examining the language we use and our preferred methods of learning. Shaw and Hawes (1998) suggest the following characterisation of the three types.

Visually-oriented learners use phrases like, 'I see what you mean', 'That looks like a good idea'.

They respond well to:

- the written word
- diagrams
- pictures

- videos.

Auditorily-oriented learners use phrases like, 'That rings a bell', 'That sounds like a good idea'.

They respond well to:

- the spoken word
- lectures
- audio-tapes
- discussion.

Kinaesthetically-oriented learners use phrases like, 'I've got the hang of this', 'That feels right to me'.

They respond well to:

- movement
- hands-on activities
- design/creative activities
- role-play/drama.

This diagnosis of sensory preferences can provide you with clues about the optimum method of diagnosing and planning your future professional development needs.

We are now going to link these sensory preferences with creative methods of undertaking CPD so that you can expand your choice of methods when preparing your CPD plan.

You can either choose the methods linked to your current sensory preference or, if you want to develop another preference, you could experiment with that.

CPD FOR VISUALLY-ORIENTED LEARNERS

Visually-oriented learners respond particularly well to diagrams and pictures. Symbols and images engage the right side of our brain and so encourage us to examine situations in a spatial and holistic way. When we use colour as part of our analysis and planning to highlight and further define issues, we are also making our results more visually memorable and this encourages long-term retention of the material.

Analysis using Rich Pictures

The method of diagnosis using Rich Pictures was developed as a part of soft systems methodology (Checkland, 1999).

Rich Pictures are not about art or aesthetics. They are a diagnostic tool that provides a process for gathering, sifting and interpreting data to assist in the fuller appreciation of a complex situation. Naughton (1985, p 31) comments:

> **Since the process of a Rich Picture is essentially a process of gathering, sifting and interpreting data (what some people call appreciating a situation), it is essentially a subjective business. That means that there is no such thing as a "correct" picture.**

The construction of a Rich Picture is a subjective 'snapshot' of both the fixed elements of a situation and the activities being carried out within it. It may look something like a cartoon with stick people, speech bubbles, images and dialogue. Figure 13 illustrates an extract from a Rich Picture of an HR trainer.

Figure 13   *Extract from a Rich Picture of an HR trainer*

A typical CPD Rich Picture may depict the developer in their current professional role and illustrate the elements of this role that they enjoy and find empowering, and the elements that they find constraining and uninspiring.

The technique could also be used to explore the elements of a future potential professional role that a developer is interested in, to assess whether the role would be a good match for their interests, skills and experience.

Planning using Learning Maps

Mind-maps or spider diagrams appeal to the creative right side of our brain which thinks spatially, responds to images and looks holistically at situations.

Rose (2000) uses the term Learning Map, and explains:

> **A Learning Map is a tool to turn ideas and facts into an easily remembered VISUAL pattern of words. You can jump from one cluster to another and literally 'see' the connection between one idea and another. It is also a tool to allow you to create a logical order for those ideas.**

The advantages of Learning Maps are:

- the information is all on one page

- everything is stripped away except key words and images

- ideas can be grouped together in clusters

- lines or arrows can be drawn to represent connections between ideas

- using a range of colours, symbols and pictures makes each Learning Map unique and more memorable.

Figure 14 illustrates an extract of a Learning Map of an HR manager.

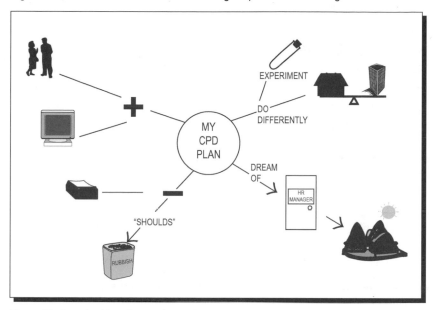

Figure 14   *Learning Map of an assistant HR manager*

Making your own Learning Map

1   Use the paper horizontally and use only one side of the paper – so you can post your Learning Map somewhere where you can look at it often.

2   Start in the centre and represent the theme of your map in a picture, symbol or phrase – eg 'My CPD'.

3   Think of the main ideas associated with your topic and identify key words – express these with pictures, symbols, words or short phrases around the central theme. Use a range of colours.

4   Stop and think – put question marks around things you don't fully understand or know; draw lines to represent connections between ideas.

5   Identify realisations, conclusions and planned actions in different colours.

6   Redraw your map if it gets messy and crowded – this is a good way to help it stick in your long-term memory.

7   Keep experimenting with this technique and use it for a variety of purposes – eg taking notes in meetings – until it becomes familiar and natural.

TUNING IN FOR AUDITORILY-ORIENTED LEARNERS

Auditorily-oriented learners respond well to the spoken word and discussion. They would benefit from working with others, either in a one-to-one dialogue – eg with a mentor, friend or learning partner – or through discussion in an action learning set or self-development group (see Chapter 8).

We suggest that you work with someone else as you experiment with the following methods.

Analysis using stories

We often use stories to help us make sense of the world or as a way of explaining our interpretation of a situation to another.

An employee in a large public sector organisation was describing her view of the pending reorganisation at her place of work using terms from J. K. Rowling's Harry Potter fantasy world. She attributed the names of the houses at Hogwarts school to different departments. She said that thinking of her place of work in these terms helped her not to take the plans for reorganisation too seriously. It was also a subtle comment about how realistic she considered these proposals to be.

Gold (1996) recognises that stories can also be an important reflective technique. He suggests that, rather than using someone else's story to assist in developing your understanding, you create your own story and tell it to another person as a narrative. Your learning partner can then help you to deepen your insight through discussion and development of your story.

In adapting Gold's work to assist you in exploring your future CPD needs, we have sequenced the process into a number of stages:

- Identify a situation that you want to explore with your learner partner.
- Examine the situation by telling a story.
- Tell the story as a narrative, describing the situation as you currently see it.
- Introduce the key characters.
- Highlight the main issues and features.
- Describe what obstacles you might encounter and how you can overcome them.
- Prompt your learning partner to ask probing and challenging questions.
- Develop a range of possible ways forward.

One HR professional, Charles, was faced with a difficult career decision. He had spent three years in a developing country as a trailing spouse while his wife carried out a high-profile secondment. By the end he had found some good work to do in the country they had been in, but then they returned and he had difficulty all over again in taking up the traces of his career in the UK. Just having re-established himself, his wife was offered an even more prestigious overseas three-year job. Charles had been just a year in his high-profile job with a local authority, working closely with the new chief executive on policy issues and programme development. He found himself resisting the disruption of moving abroad again.

Engaging in dialogue and sharing his story with a fellow learner enabled him to look at all the possible options open to him and to realise that 'I can support my wife in going to China.' When his wife picked him up at the station, after this discussion, he told her of this new sense that had come upon him, and she asked, 'Have you had a bad day at the office?' He said that it wasn't that – just a change in his sense of his own interest. They decided together to commit to going. A week later Charles's ally, the chief executive, was sacked.

By staying in touch with his feelings, discussing them with someone else and reporting them as they changed, Charles had helped himself and his wife to make an appropriate decision just at the right time. The world often rewards this flexible, grounded action.

Establishing a dialogue with a learning partner can help to look at all sides of an issue. In Charles's case he was reminded of the downside of working in large organisations – there can be boredom and stress at the same time. Going off and making a new life offers an exciting respite from this poisonous combination.

His learning partner also gently reminded him that the chief challenge that any of us face in a new situation will be that we have taken ourselves with us when we move. So whatever we have failed to face and deal with in managing our own lives will still be there to greet us when we arrive at our next stopping point.

Planning using metaphor

We have used metaphor to increase our understanding in Chapters 2 and 3. The process of using metaphor involves us in the comparison of one thing in terms of another – eg picturing our future as a roundabout. The insights we get from this pairing can help us develop our ideas. Figure 15 overleaf illustrates how Helen has used this metaphor to develop her ideas.

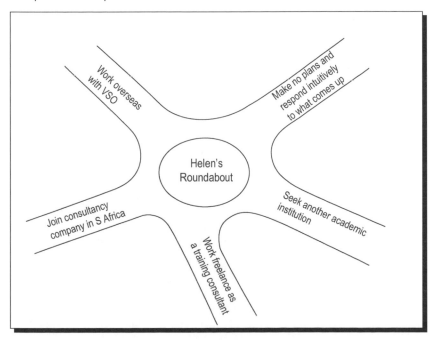

Figure 15 *Planning using the metaphor of a roundabout*

We shall describe this process of metaphorical comparison.

1   Imagine yourself standing at a roundabout.

2   Draw the number of possible exits that you think you can take at the moment – even the most unlikely.

3   Ask a friend, partner, or mentor to work with you on this exercise as they may spot possible roads that you haven't considered.

4   Now think about each possible road/exit in turn:

   ■ There may be a road linked to what you wanted to do when young but your parents/carers thought this was impractical or impossible because of lack of funds or lack of 'suitability'.
   ■ There may be a road linked to recurring dreams or fantasies.
   ■ There may be a road that involves you in more risk or unknown factors than you face at present.
   ■ There may be a well-defined road which you have been on for some time which feels as 'comfy as an old pair of slippers'.
   ■ There may be a road that your intuition is urging you to follow, but which other people say is not in your interests.

5   Metaphorically, walk up each road and explore the possibilities of this way forward.

6   Recognise that you do not need to move forward on any of the routes at the moment – you can sit and rest until a way becomes clear.

7   It is sufficient at present to recognise that you have alternatives open to you. Note down the range of routes you could follow below:

   Route 1
   Route 2
   Route 3
   Route 4
   Route 5

8   It is worth remembering at this point that our future is not a puzzle to which there is one right answer. The process of continuing professional development is about looking at all possible options and choosing the most appropriate one. It may be that some of the possible options are linked.

9   Note down positives and negatives of each potential route.

10   Also go by feel and gut reaction – some routes may feel safe or sensible, but do they feel exciting? What stirs your energy?

11   Now put a large cross at the beginning of all the roads you don't want to go down.

12   When you are left with two or more routes, develop the appropriate number of different possible future scenarios and go and research each of them further.

GETTING A HOLD ON KINAESTHETICALLY-ORIENTED LEARNING

Kinaesthetically-oriented learners respond well to movement, hands-on activities and design/creation activities. They are stimulated by activities that are tactile and use two- or three-dimensional objects.

Analysis using modelling

The process of modelling involves using objects – eg pebbles, plastic cups or Russian dolls – to set out or model a situation as you see it at the present moment.

This is a powerful diagnostic process as it allows a person to have an overview of a situation and to see it at a distance, rather than merely imagining it in their mind's eye.

Figure 16 illustrates a model of Damien's working environment as a new member of the training team.

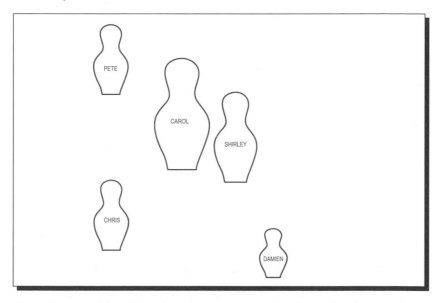

Figure 16   Model of Damien's working environment as a new member of the training team

Russian dolls, which stack one inside the other, were used for this model. They have certain advantages over the use of pebbles or paper cups, as it is possible to vary size according to how powerful each of the people feels in relation to one another. The distance between the dolls indicates the strength of relationships within the training team – the shorter the distance, the stronger the link.

When a model of the present dynamics has been created, the next challenge is to work out how you would like things to be in the future.

Figure 17 illustrates how Damien would like the dynamics of the training team to be in the future. Carol, as the team leader, still remains larger. Other members of the team are all the same size and equidistant from Carol.

Damien now has to work out what he, or others, could do differently in order to create his preferred model in reality.

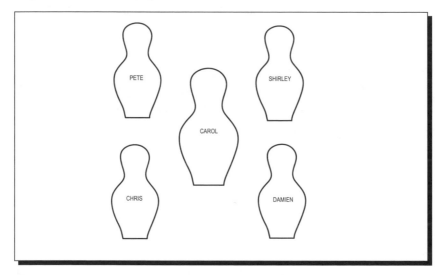

Figure 17   *Model of how Damien would like the dynamics of the training to be*

Planning using Post-It brainstorming

Having identified how you would like things to be different, the next step is to identify what you can do to bring about these changes.

A kinaesthetic way of doing this is to use Post-Its and large sheets of flipchart paper.

1   Start by writing down all your ideas for change – one idea per Post-It.

2   Post all of the completed Post-Its on a sheet of flipchart paper.

3   Group Post-Its into themes or possible solutions.

4   Create headings for the themes or possible solutions using different-coloured Post-Its.

5   Arrange themes/solutions in order of priority.

Place your completed plan where you can view it frequently. You can then remove each Post-It once you have achieved that goal. As you do this, you have both visual and kinaesthetic reminders that you are making progress towards achieving your CPD plan.

Figure 18 illustrates part of a Post-It brainstorm for a learning and development manager.

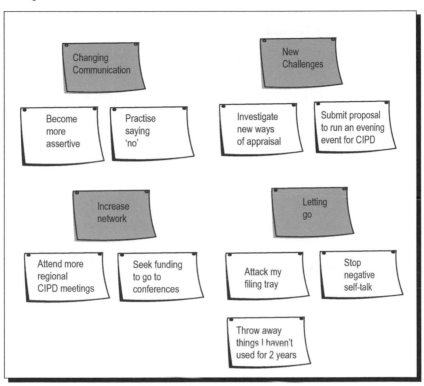

Figure 18   *Part of a Post-It brainstorm for a Learning and Development manager*

Activity

CLARIFYING YOUR SENSORY PREFERENCE AND EXPERIMENTING WITH NEW WAYS OF CREATING YOUR CPD PLAN

Having explored the different sensory preferences and the range of different ways of diagnosing and planning your CPD needs, consider:

What is your sensory preference or preferences? Which of the new methods of analysing and planning your CPD appeal to you? Identify when you are going to experiment with these methods.

FURTHER REFINING OUR SKILLS IN ANALYSIS AND PLANNING

If we are to sustain our motivation for CPD we need to be continually developing our diagnostic skills. We can do this in at least four ways, by:

1   creating a steady focus and intensifying our experience

2   improving our decision-making through linking to our intuition

3   widening our blinkers and being 'in flow'

4   keeping interested in, and open to, new experiences.

Creating a steady focus and intensifying our experience

If we are seeking insight into a situation and want to gain some penetrative understanding and wisdom, there are five mental events that can help us:

- *interest* – aspiration, eagerness, desire to be involved

- *resolve* – absence of doubt, commitment to act on that interest

- *mindfulness* – the act of holding one's intentions always in mind; being aware of the bigger context

- *concentration* – absence of ambivalence, one-pointed attention

- *wisdom* – penetrative insight, seeing deeply into a situation.

John Jeffrey (2002) helps us to appreciate that these mental events are in a hierarchy in the sense that each stage arises from and builds on the previous event.

He suggests that we use this knowledge to check our experience and establish what needs to be done to intensify our engagement in a chosen activity.

We have used this process to help us to keep focused on writing this book, when we were beset by many other demands and distractions. We found it helpful to identify which of the five mental events we found ourselves engaged in, on a particular day or time. We then worked out what we needed to do differently in order to progress to the next level.

Activity

EXPERIMENT WITH STEADYING FOCUS AND INTENSIFYING EXPERIENCE

Give full attention and follow this process when you are, for example, listening to music, reading this book or engaging in a conversation.

Notice how the experience is different as compared to when you have not focused your attention fully.

Practise going through the process in a conscious way, so that you regularly engage in this deepening experience.

Improving our decision-making through linking to our intuition

In our busy, goal-directed world it is sometimes difficult to make time to listen to our inner guidance. We may not be in a position to stop everything we are doing for a day, but if we take just ten minutes to listen to our intuition on a regular basis, we may encounter impressive results.

> **I came back from work one day and knew that I had to change my job. So I got on the Internet, found an attractive job and applied for it. As I went through two interviews I had a strong sense that this job was for me and would be offered to me. I don't get these feelings often, but I know when I do, I need to act on them.**

This is one successful manager's description of how she intuitively progressed her career. Prior to this pivotal day she had been working with a mentor clarifying her dream for the future and reflecting on her current managerial role. This in-depth reflection assisted her to both listen to her inner guidance and be ready to take action when the time felt appropriate.

What do we mean by intuition? A dictionary (Fitzpatrick, 1983, p 662) defines intuition as:

> **The power of the mind by which it immediately perceives the truth of things without reasoning or analysis.**

Tim Piering (1991, p 331) describes this as 'deep inner guidance' and makes a distinction between that and what he refers to as 'the radio voice' in each of us which is also broadcasting inner advice to us. He characterises the differences between the two to assist us to be aware of which guidance system we are tapping into.

Radio voice	Deep inner guidance
It seems to be on the surface	It seems to come from the deep
It's nervous and flighty	It's relaxing and solid
It often induces fear	It often induces tranquillity
It chatters	It has a slower deeper rhythm
The thoughts fly by	The thoughts permeate
You react	You're deliberate

It has spiritual component	It feels spiritual
The situation looks confusing	The situation looks clear
It may be more in your head	It may seem to be all over
It is gross and loud	It is subtle and quiet
It comes and goes	It doesn't leave
You're not sure it is right	You know it's right
It may have lower motives	It has the highest motives
It is restricting, boxed-in	It is expanding, evolving
It is expedient, short-term	It is long-term
It may not serve everybody	It wants the highest good for everybody

Some people identify their 'radio voice' because it sounds like a parent, relative or teacher from their past trying to control. They comment that it takes persistence and practice to sideline this voice so that they can identify and listen to their deeper, quieter inner guidance.

Many people use their inner guidance in making decisions but often don't like to admit to it. A colleague spent a day on an interview panel for a chief executive and surmised that maybe the presentations, techniques and competency frameworks we use are a way of checking, reassuring ourselves that the panel's shared intuitive choice is the right one.

Activity

CONSIDER HOW OFTEN YOU LISTEN OUT FOR, OR RESPOND TO, AN INNER URGING

Pause for a moment and

1   Think of times when you have listened to and responded to your intuition – your deep inner guidance.

2   Now recall times when you have ignored or gone against your intuitive or 'gut' feelings, or listened to your 'radio voice'.

3   Consider the outcomes from 1 and 2 – how do they differ?

Widening our blinkers and being 'in flow'

When events manifest with least effort at the most appropriate time, Csikszentmihalyi (1992) calls this 'flow'. Our own view is that when we are in flow, our lives take on the following characteristics:

- We have a zest for living.
- When we wake we can't wait to get on with our day.
- We achieve a lot without a sense of great effort or struggle.
- We have no regrets.
- We are doing what we want to do.

■   We value what we can give to the organisations and communities we serve; others appreciate and value our contribution.

Julia Cameron (1995) links this to operating from her purpose. She argues that she knows when she is 'on purpose' as synchronicity increases – people appear in her life, or events occur at just the right time to help her to progress her ideas.

If we are following a plan rigidly, or are too tired and stressed to focus beyond the next task, then we may not register these coincidences or take the initiative to respond. The challenge for us is not to be blinkered, so that we can spot such opportunities when they arrive and also have the courage to act upon them.

CONCLUSION

When we are working with people on courses and in mentoring relationships we often share the following perspective from Philip Rack (1979, 20.06):

> ### The Right Place to Be
>
> Some of us have a clear sense of what is right and wrong, for themselves personally if not for everyone else. They have a reassuring certitude and steadiness which can serve as a reference point by which others can navigate.
>
> There are others who live in a state of uncertainty, constantly rethinking their responses to changing circumstances, trying to hold on to what seems fundamental but impelled to reinterpret, often unsure where lies the boundary between the fundamental and the interpretation ...
>
> Please be patient, those of you who have found a rock to stand on, with those of us who haven't and with those of us who are not even looking for one. We live on the wave's edge, where sea, sand and sky are all mixed up together: we are tossed head over heels in the surf, catching only occasional glimpses of any fixed horizon. Some of us stay there from choice because it is exciting and it feels like the right place to be.

Vivien is a sculptor and used this quote as the basis for a stone carving. Working kinaesthetically on this theme reinforced, for her, the constancy of change – for, over time, rocks are worn away by waves.

The biggest constraint to our CPD is often ourselves. We can change – if we choose to – and in doing so we can discover that the wave's edge is the right place to be.

A Czech HR consultant agrees – her eyes light up in response to the possibility of new experiences; she regards change as 'the spice of life'.

Flexibility and challenge are both crucial in the process of CPD. We need to keep ourselves constantly fizzing in the stretch zone to avoid the danger of complacency.

We are required to do CPD for our professional association and we need to do it for ourselves. CPD can be exciting, transformative and fun – it adds 'spice' to our lives and impetus to our careers.

REFERENCES

CAMERON, J. (1997) *The artist's way: a course in discovering and recovering your creative self*. London: Pan.

CHECKLAND, P. (1999) *Soft systems methodology in action [includes a 30-year retrospective]*. Chichester: Wiley.

CSIKSZENTMIHALYI, M. (1992) *Flow: the psychology of happiness*. London: Rider.

GOLD, J. (1996) Telling stories to find the future. *Career Development International*. Vol 1, No 4, July. pp33–37.

KIRKPATRICK, E. (ed). (1983) *Chambers twentieth century dictionary*. Chambers: Edinburgh.

NAUGHTON, J. (1985) *Soft systems analysis: workbook*. Milton Keynes: Open University.

PIERING, T. (1991) *Mastery: a technology for excellence and personal evolution*. Sierra Madre, CA: Sun West.

RACK, P. (1979) In: *Quaker faith and practice*. [London]: Yearly Meeting of the Religious Society of Friends.

ROSE, C. (2000) *Master it faster: [how to learn faster, make good decisions and think creatively]*. London: Industrial Society.

SHAW, S. and HAWES, T. (1998) *Effective teaching and learning in the primary classroom: [a practical guide to brain compatible learning]*. Leicester: Optimal Learning.

www.harrypotter.com

Appendix 1

This is a case study of a senior HR professional, and has been added in the second edition of this book to provide a contrast to the example of the more junior Sandy who is mentioned throughout the text. Chris is a Divisional HR director in a large organisation. Chris's background:

- he is now in his late forties
- he has been employed in the organisation 25 years
- he is facing the threat of redundancy
- he is developing an interest in executive coaching.

CHRIS'S CPD LOG

1   Reason for doing CPD. Plateaued – bit fed up with current role. Fear of redundancy.

2   Transforming limitations. Fear that I am too old to change/won't be able to get another job.

3   Beliefs. I need the security of being employed in a large organisation

4   Metaphor. A chrysalis (but could transform into a butterfly).

5   Purpose. Helping people fulfil their potential.

6   Feedback. 1:1 interventions have been particularly successful.

7   Self-assessment metrics. MBTI – E.S.T.P. Need to be more proactive and plan my career more.

8   Organisational goals. Would like organisation to be more values-driven.

9   CIPD Core Competencies. Working as a Business Partner.

10 *World class me*. More World Class in 1:1 interventions than corporate policy?

11 *Interview myself*. Ideal job working for executive coaching organisation/ self-employed?

12 *SPICE goals*. My spirit is not much engaged in my current role AND I need to go the gym more regularly.

13 *Planned and emergent*. P = 10, E = 20. Tend to go with the flow. Have been a bit of a sleeper. Would like to be a sage.

14 *Modes*. Mode 3–4 at present. Would like to be 5–6.

15 *Widen or intensify*. One more big corporate job, or make a significant transition now?

My goals and my commitment to them

1   Develop a range of future scenarios for myself. 10.

2   Contact executive search agencies. 7.

3   Discuss my situation with Group HR director and see if there is a possibility of staying on for a limited time in my present role/similar role. 6.

4   Explore coaching/mentoring qualifications. 9.

5   Talk with local Business Link about support available for setting up as a sole trader. 5.

6   Respond to advert about executive coaching organisation. 4.

7   Get feedback from people I have helped at work. 7.

Goal	How	Success criteria	By when
1&2 Develop a range of future scenarios	Discuss with outplacement counsellor	Identified a range of future scenarios	2 months
3 Negotiate option to stay on in current role	Discuss with Group HR director	Be offered at least one other scenario as well as redundancy	Within 3 months
4 Identify appropriate qualifications needed for possible new role	Ring local universities. Contact International Coach Federation	Ascertain availability and quality of courses on offer and whether I am eligible	End of quarter
5 Find details of financial support available for small businesses	Contact local Business Link	Clarity about courses/funding/ training available and eligibility criteria	End of quarter
6 Explore option of becoming an Associate/ employee of 3 executive coaching organisations	Respond to adverts in specialist HR journals	Comparison of details with my skills and experience to judge match	Within 6 months
7 Gain feedback from people I have helped in the company	Informal conversations	Use feedback to create a list of my strengths	Within 9 months

CHRIS'S DEVELOPMENT RECORD

One year later Chris produced the following review:

Action against plan	What did I learn?	How I used this learning	Further goals
1&2 Met outplacement counsellor who helped me outline my future scenarios	Need to differentiate myself from others by deepening skills	Realisation that if made redundant had enough money for 2 years – recognition that many fears inside my own head	Information motivated me to pursue other goals outside the organisation
3 Good discussion with Group HR director	Possibility I could work another year, retain redundancy option and work a compressed 4½ day week	This could give me time to develop my next move/study for more qualifications	More motivation to pursue goals 4–7
4 Exploring professional development	Decided wanted to pursue Master's option rather than solely skills-based programme	Tried to apply for Master's programme but full this year	Apply next year. Look at Master's programmes within UK with flexible delivery
5 Talk with Business Link	Grants available for equipment for new Sole Traders. Also free training in Business and IT	Started thinking about possible business/equipment needs/premises, etc	Start with European Computer Driving Licence training (free)
6 Responded to adverts about Executive coaching	Contacted coaching organisations our company has used	Executive coaching becoming increasingly popular	Look out for other coaching organisations that may be a good match for my skills
7 Gained feedback from people I have helped in the organisation	People valued my attention to detail and thoroughness	Reconsider an HR director's role in another organisation (which is more values-driven)	Identify which organisations would be most compatible with my knowledge skills and experience

Appendix 2

THE CIPD'S EIGHT QUESTIONS, WITH COMMENTARY BY THE AUTHORS

LAST YEAR	NEXT YEAR
■ What were the three most important things you learned last year? How did you learn them? *Include either/both planned and emergent learnings. Use notes, diaries, appraisals to recall the whole year*	■ How do you identify your learning and development needs? *These could be needs against a competency framework (eg the CIPD's thinking practitioner statements), a curriculum (eg the CIPD's PDS), needs emerging from performance review, or aspirations, dreams or intentions*
■ What value did you add (to your organisation, clients or colleagues) through professional development? *Make a link between experiences, learning and actions*	■ What are your three main development objectives and how will you achieve them? *What will be different when you have achieved each?*
■ What were the tangible outcomes of your professional development in the last 12 months? *Describe how the things you did led to outcomes*	■ What differences do you plan to make (to your role, organisation, clients or colleagues)? *What will you be able to do as a consequence?*
■ Has anyone else gained from your professional development? How? *Consider beneficial impact on those indirectly involved*	■ What arrangements will you make to next review your professional development needs? *This can include when, but also how – what existing documents or specific notes you will use; anyone you will involve*

Resources and bibliography

USEFUL CONTACTS

The CIPD's CPD advisers for 1:1 support in your area. Check your branch newsletter or activities programme, for contact details of your local adviser.

The CPD helpline at CIPD headquarters: 020 8612 6622.

The CIPD's library and information line: 020 8612 6210

BIBLIOGRAPHY

ARGYRIS, C. (1991) Teaching smart people how to learn. *Harvard Business Review.* Vol 69, No 3, May-June. pp99–109.

BELBIN, R.M. (1981) *Management teams: why they succeed or fail.* London: Heinemann.

BELBIN, R.M. (1993) *Team roles at work.* Oxford: Butterworth-Heinemann.

BERG, I.K. and SZABO, P. (2005) *Brief coaching for lasting solutions.* New York: W.W. Norton.

BLYTH, A. (2000) Count the value not the hours. *The Architects' Journal.* Vol 53, 17 February.

BOLTON, G. (2001) *Reflective practice: writing and professional development.* London: Paul Chapman.

BOYDELL, T. and LEARY, M. (1996) *Identifying training needs.* London: Institute of Personnel and Development.

BUCHANAN, D. and HUCZYNSKI, A. (1997) *Organizational behaviour: an introductory text.* 3rd ed. London: Prentice Hall.

BURCHER, P.G., LEE, G.L. and SOHAL, A.S. (2005) A cross-country comparison of careers in logistics management in Australia and Britain. *International Journal of Logistics Management.* Vol 16, No 2. pp205–217.

CAMERON, J. (1997) *The artist's way: a course in discovering and recovering your creative self.* London: Pan.

CANFIELD, J. (1991) *Self-esteem and peak performance [audio cassette].* Milton Keynes: Careertrack tapes.

CHECKLAND, P. (1999) *Soft systems methodology in action [includes a 30-year retrospective].* Chichester: Wiley.

CHARTERED INSTITUTE OF PERSONNEL AND DEVELOPMENT (2006) *Fresh thinking on CPD.* London: CIPD.

CHOPRA, D. (1996) *The seven spiritual laws of success: a practical guide to the fulfilment of your dreams.* London: Bantam.

CLUTTERBUCK, D. (1998) *Learning alliances: tapping into talent.* London: Institute of Personnel and Development.

CLUTTERBUCK, D. and MEGGINSON D. (1999) *Mentoring executives and directors.* Oxford: Butterworth-Heinemann.

CLUTTERBUCK, D. and MEGGINSON, D. (2005) *Making coaching work: creating a coaching culture.* London: Chartered Institute of Personnel and Development.

CORFIELD, T. (1998) *An evaluation of the introduction and application of personal development plans at Commercial Union.* [Unpublished MSc dissertation]. Sheffield: Sheffield Business School.

COVEY, S. (1989) *The seven habits of highly effective people: restoring the character ethic.* New York: Simon and Schuster.

CSIKSZENTMIHALYI, M. (1992) *Flow: the psychology of happiness.* London: Rider.

CUNNINGHAM, I. (1999) *The wisdom of strategic learning: the self-managed learning solution.* 2nd ed. Aldershot: Gower.

FOUCAULT, M. (1978) *The history of sexuality: vol 1: an introduction.* New York: Pantheon Books.

FOWLER, A. (1996) How to manage your own CPD. *People Management.* Vol 2, No 21, 24 October. pp54–56.

FRIEDMAN, M. and ROSENMAN, R.H. (1974). *Type A behaviour and your heart.* New York: Knopf.

FRITCHIE, R. (1990) Biography work: the missing part of career development. *Industrial and Commercial Training.* Vol 22, No 2. pp27–31.

GARVEY, B. and WILLIAMSON, B. (2002) *Beyond knowledge management: dialogue, creativity and the corporate curriculum.* Harlow: Financial Times/Prentice Hall.

GERGEN, K.J. (1999) *An invitation to social construction.* London: Sage.

GIBB, S. and MEGGINSON, D. (1999) Employee development in Commercial & General Union. In: REDMAN, T. and WILKINSON, A. (eds). *Contemporary human resource management: text and cases.* Harlow: Financial Times/Prentice Hall.

GOLD, J. (1996) Telling stories to find the future. *Career Development International.* Vol 1, No 4, July. pp33–37.

GOLEMAN, D. (1996) *Emotional intelligence: why it can matter more than IQ.* London: Bloomsbury.

GOLEMAN, D. (1998) *Working with emotional intelligence.* London: Bloomsbury.

GREENLEAF, R.K., FRICK, D.M.(ed) and SPEARS, L.C. (ed) (1996) *On becoming a servant leader: the private writing of Robert K. Greenleaf.* San Francisco, CA: Jossey Bass.

HAMBLIN, A. (1974) *Evaluation of control of training.* Maidenhead: McGraw-Hill.

HANDY, C. (1994) *The empty raincoat: making sense of the future.* London: Hutchinson.

HARRISON, R. (1995) *The collected papers of Roger Harrison.* Maidenhead: McGraw-Hill.

HARROLD, F. (2001) *Be your own coach.* London: Hodder and Stoughton.

HAWKINS, P. (1999) *The art of building windmills.* Liverpool: Graduate into Employment Unit.

HERRIOT, P. (1995) The management of careers. In: TYSON, S. (ed). *Strategic prospects for human resource management.* London: Institute of Personnel and Development. pp184–205.

HILLMAN, J. (1996) *The soul's code: in search of character and calling.* London: Bantam.

HIRSCH.S. and KISE,J. (2000) *Introduction to type and coaching.* Palo Alto, CA: Consulting Psychologists Press.

HONEY,P. (1994) Establishing a learning regime. *Organisations and People.* Vol 1, No 1. pp6–9.

HONEY,P. (1998) *Live and let learn [video].* Maidenhead: Peter Honey.

IBARRA, H. (2002) How to stay stuck in the wrong career. *Harvard Business Review.* Vol. 80, No 12, December. pp40–48.

INCOMES DATA SERVICES (1999) *Career management.* IDS Study, No 678. London: Incomes Data Services.

INDUSTRIAL RELATIONS SERVICES (1998) *Learning Strategies.* January, Issue 8. London: IRS.

INGLIS, S. (1994) *Making the most of action learning.* Aldershot: Gower.

JACKSON, R. and McKERGOW, M. (2002) *The solutions focus; the simple way to positive change.* London: Nicholas Brealey.

JACQUES, R. (1996) *Manufacturing the employee: management knowledge from the 19th to the 21st centuries.* London: Sage.

KANTER, R. M. (1988) Managing change: *Dr Kanter plays Atlanta. [video].* London: BBC Enterprises.

KIRKPATRICK, E. (ed). (1983) *Chambers twentieth century dictionary.* Chambers: Edinburgh.

KLINE, N. (1999) *Time to think: listening to ignite the human mind.* London: Cassell.

KOESTLER, A. (1970) *The act of creation.* London: Pan.

LAVE, J. and WENGER, E. (1991) *Situated learning: legitimate peripheral participation.* Cambridge: Cambridge University Press.

LOCHER, K. and VAN DER BRUG, J. (1997) *Workways: seven stars to steer by.* Stroud: Hawthorn.

LUFT, J. (1984) *Group processes: an introduction to group dynamics.* Mountain View: CA: Mayfield.

LUNDIN, S., CHRISTENSEN, J. and PAUL, H. (2002) *Fish! Tales.* London: Hodder and Stoughton.

MANN, P., PRITCHARD, S. and RUMMERY, K. (2004) Supporting organisational partnerships in the public sector. *Public Management Review.* Vol 6, No 3. pp417–439.

MASLOW, A. (1943) A theory of human motivation. In: BUCHANAN, D. and HUCZYNSKI, A. (1997) *Organizational behaviour: integrated readings.* Hemel Hempstead: Prentice Hall. pp45–61.

MEGGINSON, D. (1994) Planned and emergent learning: a framework and a method. *Managing Learning.* Vol 7, No 6, June. pp29–32.

MEGGINSON, D. (1996) Planned and emergent learning: consequences for development. *Management Learning.* Vol 27, No 4. pp411–428.

MEGGINSON, D. (2001) *Research as personal unfolding.* Seminar series paper, No 4. Salford: University of Salford. Revans Institute for Action Learning.

MEGGINSON, D. and BOYDELL, T. (1979) *A manager's guide to coaching.* London: British Association for Commercial and Industrial Education.

MEGGINSON, D. and CLUTTERBUCK, D. (1995) *Mentoring in action.* London: Kogan Page.

MEGGINSON, D., CLUTTERBUCK, D. and GARVEY, B. (2006) *Mentoring in action.* 2nd ed. London: Kogan Page.

MEGGINSON, D. and PEDLER, M. (1992) *Self-development: a facilitator's guide.* Maidenhead: McGraw-Hill.

MEGGINSON, D. and WHITAKER, V. (1996) *Self-development: a facilitator's guide.* Maidenhead: McGraw-Hill.

MOSS KANTER, R. (1998) 'Dr Kanter plays Atlanta'. *Business Matters.* London: IPD.

MULLIGAN, E. (1999) *Life coaching: change your life in seven days.* London: Piatkus.

MUMFORD, A. (1997) *Management development: strategies for action.* 3rd ed. London: Institute of Personnel and Development.

NAUGHTON, J. (1985) *Soft systems analysis: workbook.* Milton Keynes: Open University.

NEATHEY, F. and SUFF, P. (1998) *Learning strategies.* IRS Management Review, No 8. London: Industrial Relations Services.

ORAM, M. and WELLINS, R. (1995) *Re-engineering's missing ingredient: the human factor.* London: Institute of Personnel and Development.

PALMER, H. (1995) *The enneagram in love and work: understanding your intimate and business relationships.* New York: HarperSanFrancisco.

PEDLER, M. (1996) *Action learning for managers.* London: Lemos and Crane.

PEDLER, M. and ASPINWALL, K. (1998) *A concise guide to the learning organization.* London: Lemos and Crane.

PEDLER, M. and BOYDELL, T. (1999) *Managing yourself.* New ed. London: Lemos and Crane.

PEDLER, M., BURGOYNE, J. and BOYDELL, T. (1994) *A manager's guide to self-development.* 3rd ed. London: McGraw-Hill.

PEDLER, M., BURGOYNE, J. and BOYDELL, T. (1997) *The learning company: a strategy for sustainable development.* 2nd ed. Maidenhead: McGraw-Hill.

PERVIN, L.A. (1989) *Goal concepts in personality and social psychology.* Hillsdale, NJ: Lawrence Erlbaum Associates.

PIERING, T. (1991) *Mastery: a technology for excellence and personal evolution.* Sierra Madre, CA: Sun West.

RACK, P. (1979) In: *Quaker faith and practice.* [London]: Yearly Meeting of the Religious Society of Friends.

REVANS, R.R. (1998) *ABC of action learning.* London: Lemos and Crane.

ROSE, C. (2000) *Master it faster: [how to learn faster, make good decisions and think creatively].* London: Industrial Society.

ROTHWELL, A. and ARNOLD, J. (2005) How HR professionals rate continuing professional development. *Human Resource Management Journal.* Vol 15, No 3. pp18–32.

SADLER-SMITH, E., ALLINSON C. W. and HAYES, J. (2000) Learning preferences and cognitive style: some implications for continuing professional development. *Management Learning.* Vol 31, No 2, pp239–256.

SANKAR, V. (2003) Big Brother is watching (your CPD). *British Medical Journal.* Vol 327, No 7413, 11 October. p855.

SCHEIN, E.H. (1980) *Organizational psychology.* 3rd ed. Englewood Cliffs, NJ: Prentice Hall.

SCHON, D.A. (1991) *The reflective practitioner: how professionals think in action.* Aldershot: Ashgate.

SENGE, P. (1990) The leader's new work: building learning organizations. *Sloan Management Review.* Vol 32, No 1. pp7–23.

SENGE, P. (1992) *The fifth discipline: the art and practice of the learning organization.* London: Century Business.

SENGE, P., ROBERTS, C. and ROSS, R.B. (1994) *The fifth discipline fieldbook: strategies and tools for building a learning organization.* London: Nicholas Brealey.

SHAW, S. and HAWES, T. (1998) *Effective teaching and learning in the primary classroom: [a practical guide to brain compatible learning].* Leicester: Optimal Learning.

STRANDGAARD, F. (1981) *NLP made visual.* Copenhagen: Connector.

TAMKIN, P., BARBER, L. and HIRSH, W. (1995) *Personal development plans: case studies of practice.* Brighton: Institute for Employment Studies.

VAN JAARSVELD, D. and BATT, R. (2002) Changes in employment and working conditions among technical and professional workers. *Proceedings of the 54th Annual Meeting of the Industrial Relations Research Association.* Madison, WI: Industrial Relations Research Association.

WARR, P., BIRD, M. and RACKHAM, N. (1970) *Evaluation of management training: a practical framework, with cases, for evaluating training needs and results.* London: Gower.

WEICK, K.E. (1995) *Sensemaking in organizations.* Thousand Oaks, CA: Sage.

WHITAKER, V. (1994) *Managing people.* London: HarperCollins.

WHITAKER, V. (1995) Networking. In: CRAINER, S. (ed). *The Financial Times handbook of management.* London: Pitman.

WILLIAMSON, M. (1996) *A Return to Love: Reflections on the Principles of a Course in Miracles.* London: Thorson.

www.cipd.co.uk

www.harrypotter.com

INDEX

action learning, 79–80, 118–21
    sets, 120–1
attitude(s) and professional progress,
    11–12
Belbin's team roles, 43–4
benchmarking, as an element in, CPD
    77–8
'Big rocks' story, 10–12
career development/progress, 3, 33–5
    and this book, xiii
    portfolio careers, 7
career metaphor(s), 34–7
    map' of, 35–6
career plateau, 33–5
causality and teleology, 23–4
change, 107–9
    and CPD, 4, 45–6, 48
Chris's log/diary/plan, see log to monitor
    CPD, Chris's
CIPD, the, 5, 21, 30, 45–8, 78–9, 89, 90,
    98, 113–14, 116, 120, 147
    and the key principles of CPD, 5,
      147
    branch activities of, 78–9, 113–14
    CPD requirement for members of,
      xiv, 5, 21, 89, 98, 147
    CPD scanner, 45–6, 48, 54
    Professional Development Scheme,
      46–7
    Professional Standards of, 45–8
    the BACKUP competencies, 46–7,
      48
    'thinking performer' and 'business
      partner' concepts, 46–7
coaching and/or mentoring, 77–8
college curriculum(s) and CPD, 4–5
competencies, as organisational metrics,
    30, 31–2, 45–6
conference-attending, as a means of
    CPD, 78–9
congruence in personal and professional
    life, 31–2, 39, 40, 103

continuing professional development
    (CPD)
    analysis of, 1, 19–21, 27, 70–1, 74–
      5, 134–41
    as a holistic process, 3, 51, 108–10
    as a journey (with a map) or as
      exploration, 24
    assessment/summary of agenda for,
      1, 51–4
    benefits of, 4–5, 7–9
    core concepts/key principles of, 3–4,
      5, 7–9
    cycle(s) of, 1, 27, 90–98
    FAQs about, 81–3
    hindrances and limitations to, 9–14
    implementing, 27, 69–85
    log to monitor progress in, 1, 48–9,
      69, 87–96, 144–5
    paradoxes within, the seven, 19–24
    prioritising, 8–10, 15, 27, 64–7, 71–2
    relevance of, 14–15
    review and evaluation of, 1, 27, 81,
      90–8
    successes/achievements in, 1, 27,
      101, 103–14
    the nature of, 3–16, 19–25
    the process of, 3
    see also development goals; devel-
      opment needs; development
      plans/planning; empowerment
      through CPD; learning; reflection;
      stakeholders in CPD
core concepts of CPD, 3–4, 7–9
course(s), as a means of CPD, 78–9
CPD cycle, the, 1, 27
critical reasoning skills, xiii
cultural influences on work attitudes, 11–
    12
curiosity as an element for CPD, 4, 25
decision-making linked to intuition, 138–
    41
    'radio voice' and inner guidance,
      139–40

development goals, 51–3, 54, 55–62, 71–2, 87–9, 96–7, 145–6
  balance in life and, 55–7
  changing, 89, 96–7
  goal-setting theory, 59–62
  prioritising, 519–64, 71–2
  recording of, 87–9, 145–6
  setting, 55–62
  SPICE framework for setting, 55–7
  testing commitment to, 64
  see also development needs; development plans/planning
development needs
  identification of, 29–49
  prioritising in order to select activities to meet, 51–68
  see also continuing professional development (CPD); development goals; world class me
development plan(s)/planning, 1, 19–25, 27, 56–9, 64–7, 88, 106–8, 127–8, 137–41, 146
  celebrating completion of, 112–13
  demonic aspect of, 106–9
  formats for, 64–7
  implementation of, 69–85
  methods for implementing, 75–81
  NLP and, 127–38
  review of, 88, 146
emergent learning, see learning, 'emergent'
employers, and CPD in respect of their employees, 4
  and this book, xiv
empowerment through CPD, 3, 120, 127–41
'excess baggage', letting go of, 109–12
'extraordinarily realistic self-image' (ERSI), 29, 30–2
  framework diagram, 31–2
feedback, as an element of CPD, 30, 40–3, 70–1, 73–5, 77–9
  lack of, 32–3
  role negotiation, 77–8
  see also 360-degree review/appraisal/feedback
'fuzziness' and lack of clear vision, correction of, 9–11
goals for development, see development goals

goal-setting theory, 59–62
  the seven modes of, 59–61
hindrances to CPD, see continuing professional development, hindrances and limitations to
HRD and HRD interventions, 4
HR managers, and this book, xiv
innovation, as an element in CPD, 70–1, 72–3
interpersonal skills, as an element in CPD, 70–1, 74–5
  the four component elements of, 74–5
intuition, linked to decision-making, 138–41
  'radio voice' and inner guidance, 139–40
Johari window, the, 38
leader and leadership, 40
learning
  action learning, 79–80, 118–21
  anticipating opportunities for, 70–2
  as part of everyday work, 5, 7–9
  capability approach to, 54
  e-learning, 79–80
  'emergent', 57–9
  informal and self-directed, 78–81
  seeking out new, 70–3, 77–8
  the skills of, 70–5
  ways/categories of, ('planned'/'emergent'; 'sleepers'/'warriors'/'adventurers'/'sages'), 56–9
learning maps, see mind maps
learning needs, analysis of, 5, 6–7
  see also development needs
lecturers' tutor manual, xiii
limitations to CPD, see continuing professional development, hindrances and limitations to
log to monitor CPD, 1, 48–9, 695, 87–96, 103–4
  as a portfolio of action and learning, 95–6
  Chris's, 144–5
  format(s) for, 89–96
  journal-/diary-writing, 90, 92–6
  learning log(s), 91
  performance log(s), 92
  Sandy's, 48–9, 63, 66–8, 69–71, 83–5, 88

success/achievement log(s), 103–4
Maslow's hierarchy, 39–40
mentoring and/or coaching, 77–8, 122–4
metaphor as basis for a development plan, 132–5
methods of development, 75–81
metrics, *see* competencies; organisational metrics; professional metrics; psychometrics; self-assessment, metrics for
mind maps, learning maps, 130–2
modelling as a means of situation analysis, 134–6
NLP, *see* neuro-linguistic programming
network(s) and networking, 1, 27, 79–80, 115–24
    analysing one's CPD network, 115–18
    creation/development of, 116–24
    types of, 115–16
neuro-linguistic programming (NLP), 127–38
    auditory orientation, 127–8, 131–5
    kinaesthetic orientation, 127–8, 134–8
    visual orientation, 127–32
organisational goals, 43–5
organisational metrics, 30, 43–6
paradoxes within CPD, *see* continuing professional development, paradoxes within, the seven
personality Types A and B (Buchanan and Huczynski), 107–8
planning CPD, *see* development plan(s)/planning
Post-It brainstorming to bring about change, 135–8
procrastination/prevarication, prevention of, 13
professional development, 5–6
    see also career development/progress; continuing professional development (CPD)
professional metrics, 30, 31–2
psychometrics, as a means of feedback, 30
questioning, as an element of CPD, 4, 147
reading, as an element in CPD, 79–80

recording one's CPD, *see* log to monitor CPD
reflection, xiii, 3, 4, 27, 29–30, 37–40, 87–98, 118–20
    logging/recording, 90–6
    phases in, 118–20
responsibility for one's own development, 3, 5, 6, 11–12, 14
retention of staff, *see* staff retention
review of one's own work/progress, 3, 81, 90–8
Rich Pictures, 128–9
risk-taking, as an element in CPD, 70–1, 72–3
role negotiation for feedback/learning, 77–8
sabbatical(s), 79–80
Sandy's log/diary/plan, *see* log to monitor CPD, Sandy's
self, sense of, 29–30, 103
self-actualisation, 39–40
self-assessment in relation to CPD, 27, 40, 74–5
    metrics for, 31–2, 40, 42–4
    personality frameworks, 42–4
self-diagnostic questionnaires, 30
seminar(s), as a means of CPD, 78–9
seven paradoxes within CPD, *see* continuing professional development, paradoxes within
shadowing, as an element in CPD, 77–8
skills deficit(s), analysis and correction of, 9–10
staff retention, CPD and, 4
stakeholders in CPD, 4–5
stories as a means of analysis, 131–5
'stretching', the stretch zone, 32–4, 55–7
students
    full-time, xiii, 21, 48, 120
    part-time, xiii, 4, 120
    see also college curriculum(s) and CPD
succession planning, CPD and, 4
team roles (Belbin), 43–4
technology, the influence of modern, 6
teleology and causality, 23–4
thanking people who have helped, 105
360-degree review/appraisal/feedback, 31–2, 41–3, 78–9
time management and CPD, 8–10

training gap, the, 54
tutor manual for lecturers, xiii
values, 111–13
    and CPD, 23–4, 39–40
work-life balance, 15, 55, 108–9

and development goals, 55–7
and development successes, 108–10
work project(s) as a means of CPD, 76–8
world class me, 51–3, 61–2, 66–7

Also from CIPD Publishing . . .

Human Resource Management in an International Context

Rosemary Lucas, Ben Lupton and Hamish Mathieson

This text considers how human resource management, policies and practices manifest themselves in organisations internationally. The text moves beyond the large organisation or multinational corporation by offering discussion about, and providing practical examples from, a wide range of organisations including public and private, small and medium-sized enterprises, and manufacturing or service-based organisations.

Order your copy now online at www.cipd.co.uk/bookstore or call us on 0870 800 3366

Rosemary Lucas is Professor of Employment Relations and Director of the Centre for Hospitality and Employment Research (CHER), Manchester Metropolitan University Business School (MMUBS).

Ben Lupton is Principal Lecturer in Human Resource Management, Manchester Metropolitan University Business School (MMUBS).

Hamish Mathieson is Senior Lecturer in Employment Relations, Manchester Metropolitan University Business School (MMUBS).

| Published 2007 | 1 84398 109 2 | Paperback | 488 pages |

The Chartered Institute of Personnel and Development is the leading publisher of books and reports for personnel and training professionals, students and all those concerned with the effective management and development of people at work.

Membership has its rewards

Join us online today as an Affiliate member and get immediate access to our member services. As a member you'll also be entitled to special discounts on our range of courses, conferences, books and training resources.

To find out more, visit www.cipd.co.uk/affiliate or call us on 020 8612 6208.